SELECTED POEMS

MICK IMLAH ∽ Selected Poems

Edited by Mark Ford
with an Introduction by Alan Hollinghurst

faber and faber

First published in 2010
by Faber and Faber Limited
Bloomsbury House
74–77 Great Russell street
London WC1B 3DA

Typeset by Faber and Faber Limited
Printed in England by T. J. International Ltd, Padstow, Cornwall

A CIP record for this book
is available from the British Library

ISBN 978-0-571-26881-8

10 9 8 7 6 5 4 3 2 1

Contents

Unpublished and Uncollected Poems

Introduction

When Mick Imlah died, in January 2009, he was mourned as one of the outstanding British poets of his time. He published only two collections, both dazzlingly original though very different in mood. *Birthmarks* came out in 1988, when he was thirty-one, *The Lost Leader* not till 2008, when he had been diagnosed with motor neurone disease and knew he did not have long to live. The twenty-year gap between the books, though tantalising in the extreme for his admirers, was revealed as a period of continuous exploration and change. For at least ten years before its publication the second book was expected, its name was chosen, it was about to be sent to a publisher – on occasion was sent, and then retracted. A few new poems appeared in *Penguin Modern Poets 3* (1995), but it was the small private-press publication *Diehard* in 2006 that gave a first real taste of his new material. The long delay, the result both of Imlah's technical perfectionism and of a steady deepening and focusing of his vision, gave an extraordinary cumulative force to the *The Lost Leader* when he finally decided to let it appear. It won the Forward Prize for the best collection of 2008, and seems already a pre-eminent book of a much longer period.

It was typical of Imlah not to be troubled by the career pressures which naturally affect most young writers. He had a sensible belief in his own gifts, but he was as indifferent to status as he was to money and to all possessions except books. The work itself was the important thing, and he had infinite patience with it. To those who knew him he seemed to move at two different speeds simultaneously. He was wonderfully quick-witted, funny, several steps ahead in exact and ironic understanding of any matter being talked about; but he was equally and happily prone to a dawdling, quizzical slowness. It was much the same in his physical movements. In his Oxford days he was a very fast runner; he always loved sport, cricket and rugby in particular, both of which he played for Magdalen College, captaining the First XV in 1978. He played on the wing, where he showed a thrilling power of acceleration. But off the pitch his preferred pace was a gentle amble. He stayed on a long time in Oxford, teaching, writing poems, working on a never-finished doctoral thesis on King Arthur in Victorian poetry. I can see him very clearly now, leaving Magdalen and sauntering up the High Street, looking about him in his friendly but slightly abstracted fashion. There was always a hint of mystery to him, a sense of speed held in reserve, of subtle and complex thought not lightly given away. He combined the instincts of the team player with those of the poetic solitary, whose life was being led, richly but unguessably, in his imagination.

His parents both came from Aberdeen, and Imlah spent the first ten years of his life in Milngavie, not far from Glasgow. But his father's work in insurance brought the family south in 1966, to West Wickham in Kent, and Imlah subsequently won a scholarship to nearby Dulwich College; the poems and stories he wrote there, mixed up in notebooks with lists of pop songs and cricket scores (two lasting obsessions), gave early evidence of his sardonic humour and eye for the surreal. From Dulwich he won a Demyship, or college scholarship, at Magdalen, going up in 1976.

From the start he was academically brilliant, in his off-beat and laconically concise way. I was a nervous junior lecturer when I first met him, my nerves not lessened by his way of turning up for a tutorial empty-handed, and after a minute or two's stilted chat producing his neatly folded essay from the back pocket of his jeans. His reserve in tutorials was largely shyness, though sometimes a tactful concealment of the fact that he knew more about the subject in question than I did. But it quickly emerged that he wrote poems, and I sometimes shared the task, generally borne by his girlfriends, of typing them up, a skill he refused to learn for himself until forced to use an office word processor in the mid-1990s. (Otherwise, everything he submitted to editors and printers was in his exemplary handwriting, clear but personal, half copperplate, half italic.) In the days before creative writing had entered university syllabuses Magdalen College provided perhaps the best academic environment for a young poet. He had John Fuller as a tutor and encourager; and Magdalen's John Florio Society, at which poems are read and criticised with at least a pretence of ignorance of their authorship, was a useful forum for Imlah's early work. For several years he was secretary of the Society, his minutes of the previous meeting becoming ever more extended and involved fantasias on the relatively ordinary things that had actually been said and done. They showed a talent for a baroque and slightly menacing transformation of reality that was also seen in many of his poems. Throughout his life, Imlah's strong feelings of loyalty to groups, teams and institutions that nurtured him coexisted with a tendency to satirical mischief and play.

In 1982 Fuller's Sycamore Press published Imlah's first pamphlet, *The Zoologist's Bath and Other Adventures*. It was a strikingly original debut, its easy acquaintance with his favourite Victorians combined with an unsettling sense of the contemporary. The presence of Browning was evident in the blank-verse dramatic monologues, the comic-horror title poem in particular being spoken by a ripely eccentric Victorian evolutionist; though that poem also has a short opening section spoken by the imaginary scientist's sister, which is the first appearance of a looser anapaestic metre which was to become a long-term favourite of Imlah's. The other poems used stanzaic forms, with an instinct for rhyme, rhythm and shape shown by few of his contemporaries. His work was literary in the most vital sense, relishing formal control and syntactical play, and rich in allusions to a hinterland of histories, real and imaginary. It wasn't simply narrative, it spoke with casual confidence of a world made of stories. He could deconstruct, condense or hallucinate a story, or merely touch on it with cool obliquity, but the narrative impulse and interest were central to his poetry from the start. He never wrote a merely descriptive poem, and even the mysterious lyric poems in *Birthmarks* involve cryptic glimpses of stories; while the little six-line verses on 'The Counties of England' visit playfully surreal histories on their helpless subjects. It was only at the end of his life that he wrote poems undisguisedly about those he loved, his partner and his children, and they too take the form of anecdotes, transfigured by feeling and an exact instinct for how feeling may be expressed.

Birthmarks dealt in part, as Imlah explained, with 'those things – class, family, congenital strengths and weaknesses, prejudices, addictions, tattoos, that people are stuck with, whether they like it or not'. One notes that the list comprises the congenital and the acquired, and that the weaknesses outnumber the strengths, while class and family have at least an ambivalent status. As he says in the poem 'Birthmark', 'it's as bad to fall astray / As to start from the wrong place'. There the bilberry-coloured stain 'stamped / From ear to livid ear' is self-induced, the result of incessant drinking; that it is called a birthmark suggests that it is nonetheless inescapable. The bizarre conceit, by which each broken vein is the lost leg of a millipede, making a symbolic self-sacrifice for the drinking poet, is treated with the unforgettable logic of a sinister dream. But if various waking nightmares – failure, sexual betrayal, the drinker's oblivion – stalk the pages of *Birthmarks*, the book itself gives no sense of entrapment, is indeed exhilaratingly inventive. On the page as on the field Imlah was a 'Classic sure-foot', as he calls the mountain goat that nonetheless falls to its death. The darkly witty placing and facing of horrors, the presaging and then the monitoring of disaster, were always to be his forte.

Part of the appeal of *Birthmarks* lay naturally in its being a young man's book, magnetised by youthful mortifications just as it was energised by a youthful pleasure in pure skill. A certain shyness or embarrassability informed the poems' story-telling, their quirky mixture of candour and deflection. To those who knew him then the book is likely to evoke, in its tones and gestures and its shades of irony, a shadow portrait of Imlah in his twenties. His early life was, in a happy and ordinary but undeniable way, fairly sheltered, and there was a vein of passivity in his temperament that showed in his dreamy slowness and sometimes uneasy deferral of decisions. He loved the reassuring routines of work, sport, smoking and drinking – the last interfering sometimes with the first. He was dynamically fit, but physically unadventurous, never learning to swim, ride a bicycle or drive a car. He would go to Scotland, or to John Fuller's cottage in North Wales with other Oxford friends, but for a long time resisted foreign travel. The announcement one year that he really was going to tour the northern French cathedrals was followed in due course by a postcard from Taunton, which was easier to get to, and where he was staying in a pub and watching the cricket (the 'twin towers' of Taunton, in his poem 'Somerset', are Ian Botham and Viv Richards). It was only when he got a job on *Departures*, the American Express travel magazine, that the post-cards started coming in from Mauritius or the Seychelles instead. All of which is perhaps only to say that inexperience was quite consciously a part of the compound of his early work. 'Experience', he suggested in an interview in 1983, 'can be confining, almost a handicap.' 'Brawl in Co. Kerry' and 'Visiting St Anthony' were what he called 'imaginary travel poems': 'Not travelling has its own glamour . . . It's the places I haven't been that are interesting to me.' In his second year at Oxford he was recycling his school essays with impressive results, and he got a very good First without bothering to read very much; as a young man he had a clever person's laziness and justifiable confidence in his own powers.

One or two peevish voices thought Imlah too clever, too dustily 'Oxonian', failing to see how mordantly modern many of the fables and instances in *Birthmarks* were, within their formal virtuosity and confidently literary bearing. The academic scaffolding around his poems was often decidedly shaky and fanciful. He had the surrealist's deadpan way of introducing impossibilities on the same footing as verified fact, and such straight-faced mischief-making runs throughout his work. 'The Zoologist's Bath' is the most systematic example, a fake history supported by fake authorities, under a fake epigraph. (The epigraph was to become a favoured device of Imlah's, often authentic, sometimes, like Walter Scott's attributions to an 'Old Play', made up: he saw that the epigraph, while seeming to prepare the reader, like the text of a sermon, might just as easily be used to bamboozle.) In the grip of his idea of reverse evolution, the zoologist, with the thoroughness and self-conviction of a certain kind of madness, sees evidence all around him of a return to the fishy state:

> I'll see a pheasant
> Issue unshelled spawn, a cow discharge
> Its mackerel in pats, a vivid worm
> Crack as the pike slides out. And suddenly

Hypotheses will rocket round my skull
Like starfish rolled by gulls across the sky;
Are not the night secretions of the tern,
For instance, like an oily saw-dust, sign
Of the discreet development of gills?

Here are several kinds of strangeness – Ernst-like metamor-phoses, Carrollian absurdities, the colourful fantasy of 'mad' and nonsense poetry – all grounded in classic blank verse, with its note of donnish excitement and precision ('Are not the night secretions of the tern . . . ?'). It gives us a slide-show that is anything but dusty, a weirdly beautiful dreamworld of queasy uncertainties. Internal echoes ('skull', 'gulls', 'gills') increase the sense of teeming interconnectedness. Imlah loves such slippages and echoes within the verbal fabric of a poem – as when in the sequence 'Mountains' the Audenesque roll-call of climbers' names ('*Viollet, Wavering, / White, Wood*') in 'Snowdonian' recur as ordinary nouns in 'Alpine' ('"Here are my hands . . . Violet and white / And hard as wood"'). The effect is uncanny, like the confirmation of something inevitable but only dimly understood.

The bravura 'Cockney' is another poem founded on un-stable mutations – some blatant (the 'disco remix of *The Dance of the Seven Veils*'), others more recondite: readers should beware, for instance, of the poem's account of the composer Gerald Finzi, 'An aristocrat who betrayed what he stood for and set up in Bow with his matchgirl fiancée' – a lie in every respect. Such twisting out of the true is of little help to the social-climbing Cockney lad, betrayed by his uncontrol-lable 'base-born vowels' and base-born behaviour at a post-concert party with 'the Previns'. (He ends up doing a striptease to that imaginary disco remix.) Yet the poem itself is a triumph of technical control, in immensely long-lined rhyming triplets, the rhymes in fact Owen-like half-rhymes but treated with Byronic panache. (The half-rhyme, with its difference-in-likeness, is aptly chosen.) In 'Goldilocks', the young academic narrator finds his smug superiority challenged but less seriously damaged by the comparable irruption of a stinking alter ego, the Scottish tramp who has stolen the bed in his college guest room. His ejection of this incubus is achieved physically with a boot, but verbally with the tongs of Jamesian irony: 'Still, the lifespan of sociable feelings is shortest of all / In the breast of the migrant Clydesider', a man of 'the sort anthropologists group in the genus of *tramp*' (itself an uncanny echo of Henry James's early story 'A Passionate Pilgrim': 'there came trudging along the road an individual whom, from afar, I recognized as a member of the genus "tramp"'). The incessant play of irony is integral to Imlah's voice as a poet, as it was to his living voice; anyone who knew him will hear in his verse those small hesitations and pushings that signalled his keen consciousness and control of tone, the instinctive placing and raising of a word to bring out its comedy, whether intrinsic or contextual. The 'donnish' tone was part of his repertoire, as were the echoes of English verse, from Shakespeare to Larkin, that are heard in the extraordinary blank verse monologue 'Solomon', published for the first time in this *Selected Poems*.

Imlah clearly had a sense of *The Lost Leader* as a whole from early on, but a lot had to happen before it reached a shape, mass and pitch he was satisfied with. An element of mystery lies in the gestation of the book and survives in the exceptionally rich and complex assemblage of the finished thing: it is a book we are only beginning to get to know. The sense of an inescapable history that is a keynote of *Birthmarks* permeates much of the collection to savage or tragic or absurd effect. In 1994 he wrote of this work in progress, 'If

Birthmarks says, we can only be what we are, this says, we can fail to be even that.' Five years later, he explained that many of the poems in it would 'investigate, some in personal but more of them in historical contexts, the separation of the individual from what he ought to belong to, whether by his own fault, by the dereliction of elders or superiors or God, or by the misdirection of false "prophets": there are Scottish and Hebrew motifs, and clutches of poems set in the eighteenth and nineteenth centuries.' The title poem was then seen as being a longer 'sequence' that would connect 'a personal and contemporary disillusion' with 'the experience of the Highland Scots deserted by Bonnie Prince Charlie after Culloden': further sections were written to do just that, but over the following years the poem was cut back, refined and redefined into the luminous masterpiece that it now is. The note of personal disillusion persists, as so often in Imlah, as an undertone rather than a subject.

'There are Scottish . . . motifs . . .' The slowness of the book's gestation was due in part to Imlah's own ramifying exploration of a subject which surprisingly he had barely touched on before. In *Birthmarks* only one parenthetical aside '(Och, if he'd known *I* was Scottish! Then I'd have got it)' alluded at all to his nationality, and that was put in the mouth of a fictional narrator. In one of the epigraphs to the poem 'Namely', his bristlingly humorous disquisition on his own unusual surname, he quotes Angus Calder, in *Scotland on Sunday*: 'Few people thought Mick Imlah, who teaches at Oxford, was a "Scottish poet".' As he admits more plainly in his moving elegy for his friend Stephen Boyd, 'years of a Southern education . . . / Had trimmed my Scottishness to a tartan phrase / Brought out on match days and Remembrance Days.' His Scottish accent was only fleetingly used, something kept up his sleeve, as he said, 'like a dirk for tight corners'. But his new collection was to be steeped in Scotland, in Scottish history and landscape, literature and legend. A series of dated episodes, and dated lives, from 'Muck' (merely 'AD', an apocryphal story of St Kevin), and 'Michael Scot' (1175–1232), through to 'Stephen Boyd' (1957–95), shapes the book, his personal narrative seeming to emerge in the last phase from this long and fractured Scottish history. The reasons for this development are inextricably both personal and professional. Imlah began to spend more and more time in Scotland, and the house of a close friend in Ayrshire became a kind of second home to him, where much reading and writing were done. At the same time he took on the editing, with Robert Crawford, of the massive *New Penguin Book of Scottish Verse* (2000), with its abundance of poems in Gaelic, and a handful of other languages, faced by distinguished English translations. (Imlah's version of the Old French 'Fergus of Galloway' was one of them, later revised for *The Lost Leader*.)

Imlah's career as an editor had begun in Oxford, when in 1983 he had been responsible, with three other friends, for reviving the long-dormant *Oxford Poetry*. In the same year he had taken over from Andrew Motion the editorship of *Poetry Review*, which he shared at first with Tracey Warr. Warr left within a year, but Imlah continued there until the summer of 1986, when he returned to Oxford for a further two years as a junior lecturer in English at his old college. After *Birthmarks* had come out, to wide acclaim, in 1988, there was a sense that he was truly launched as a poet; but for the following three years he wrote no poems at all. In fact, these were also the years that he was working as Poetry Editor at Chatto and Windus, a job into which he had again followed Motion. It was another phase in his benign but clear-eyed career as an enabler of poetry, carried on to the end through his thirteen years as Poetry Editor at the *TLS*.

He had started reviewing for the *TLS* in the early 1980s. To someone who had difficulty in releasing anything for publication, the strict demands of deadlines were oppressive but clearly beneficial. The whole process, especially once he had joined the staff of the paper in 1992 and could choose what he wanted to write about, became one of exploration, spreading and deepening. Boyish skating was replaced by wide and curious and patient reading, which seemed to become a more and more integral part of his personality, as it did of his work. The unwieldy kitbags from which he was to become almost inseparable contained alongside various kinds of sports gear the ever heavier mass of books that he wanted to keep within reach. He developed into a wonderful critic, quietly brilliant, wise and humane. Much of his best critical writing was on relatively minor writers, some of them almost forgotten, such as Robert Bridges or Laurence Binyon, some well known but less regarded, like John Buchan: subjects that brought out his canny wit as well as a kind of fraternal tenderness, and showed his complete indifference to fashion.

Reviewing was also a way of exploring Scotland, which sometimes bore very direct fruit, as in the case of Tom Leonard's *Places of the Mind* (1993), his biography of the alcoholic Scottish poet James Thomson, 'B.V.', who became the subject of the second of Imlah's 'Afterlives of the Poets' (following the tour de force of that on Tennyson, produced for his centenary the previous year). These extraordinary poems, verse medleys with prose interpolations, startlingly funny in their view of literary history and the delusions of posterity, are in a genre Imlah made his own. He placed them at the end of *The Lost Leader*, their questions about the afterlife of a poet posed with typical wit and defiance. Sir Walter Scott was another new passion, and the poem 'Diehard' is about him, a kind of essay-poem, ranging round the subject, describing

Scott himself in amusing and touching episodes and digressions, and also paying tribute to him as a novelist in a challenge to critics such as Leavis ('Who now / Reads *Anne of Geierstein?*'):

> The Scott novel's a 'Big Bow-Wow', shaggy,
> Heavy, particular; slow to rouse; but once fixed,
> Will not give up its grip on your reading leg.

Like many poems in *The Lost Leader* it bristles with learning, deployed both to disorientate and to captivate the reader.

The earlier poems in the book pay more textual homage to Scottish sources. It opens with a false start, 'Muck', one of Imlah's vaguely nightmarish quest-poems, like 'Visiting St Anthony' in *Birthmarks*. Here it is presumably a visit to St Columba on Iona that has gone astray, the episode being narrated by a monk travelling with St Kevin who mistakenly thinks they've landed on Mull, not the inhospitable Muck. The surrealism of the scene, with its closely described totemic objects (crosses? ladders? graves?), is given a postmodern twist by casual anachronisms (toy tractor, thermos) which will be a feature of the whole book. 'The Prophecies' which follow are three predictions taken from Adomnán's seventh-century *Life of Columba*, foretellings of completely unimportant things which do indeed happen, the fourth prophecy being that the saint's life by Adomnán will be written and appear in Penguin Classics in 1999 (this time he's just out – it was published there in 1995). The prophecies are presented in four sonnets, prediction in the octave, fulfilment in the sestet, but what makes the poem is its entirely prosaic tone, which invests the incidents with an air of irresistible fatuity. Something comparable, a mood of simmering absurdity just kept in check, characterises 'Braveheart', Imlah's substantial narrative poem about the attempted transport of Robert the Bruce's heart to the Holy

Land – it ends up, with the sort of bathos he relishes, squashed under a Saracen's heel at the battle of Teba. (Its subsequent journey back to its final resting place in Melrose Abbey lies in the future at the poem's end: it 'ached towards the north, trailing his pipes'.) The story is narrated in rollicking heroic couplets, neatly contained in twelve-line stanzas.

'Fergus of Galloway', Imlah's equally cheerful adaptation from the Old French *Roman de Fergus*, maintains the hectically short-winded tone of the original, while livening it up with jokes and wordplay, the result sounding like one of Belloc's *Cautionary Tales*, breaking off before the expected comeuppance. The knockout poem of this kind, though, is 'The Ayrshire Orpheus', a modernised version of eight climactic stanzas from Robert Henryson's 'Orpheus and Eurydice'. Here the mythic and the everyday come together in a specifically Scottish setting. Imlah follows Henryson's rhyme royal exactly, but with violent disjunctions of language and tone, comedy and horror. Where Henryson writes, at the climax of the poem,

> Quhat will ye moir? in schort conclusioun,
> he blent bakward, And pluto come annone,
> And on to hell with hir agane is gone.

Imlah has:

> I hate to say – she fell a yard behind –
> Backward he blinked – chains belted from the deeps
> And yanked Eurydice to Hell for keeps.

– preserving the one vital phrase, the blink backwards, and heightening the despair by his reckless violation of the decorum of the original. There follows the elegiac 'short conclusion', in which Orpheus is seen in some half-derelict Carrick town, 'dismal in the twilight of surviving': 'Alone with his shopping, sore to be rid of her, / He walks the roads of home a widower' – even the sorry shift of that imperfect rhyme adding to the effect.

No one will fail to feel the bleakness that runs through many of the poems in the book, however briskly or obliquely handled. The sardonic fatalism of much of Imlah's poetry came from a very private region of his life, often hard to square with the record of his evident success in work, love, art and sport. But equally, the poems are never confessional, and though there were certainly periods of unhappiness and confusion in his life, the reader will search in vain for an unmediated account of them in his work. It was always his belief that poems 'should somehow (whatever else they do) entertain or stimulate a reader, rather than exalting the writer'. He is indeed a wonderfully entertaining poet, and his fine judgement in such matters persists in the unprecedentedly personal final poems, 'Maren' and 'Iona', their tone, as he rightly thought, 'not mawkish . . . or maudlin'. The dramatic strategies of narrative appealed to his instinctive tact and modesty – though the drama itself might be fierce or farcical. This was clearly something that fascinated him in Tennyson, whom he had always loved more, he said, 'than most people seem to'. He made a selection of his work for Faber's Poet-to-Poet series (typically long-delayed, it appeared in 2004); in the introduction he wrote intimately of Tennyson's reticence, his problems in revealing his deepest experience to the public, when that experience was 'unsocial, painful, and shaming to a degree'. 'The "coming woe" is always large on Tennyson's horizon . . . and his poems had to put on forms or metaphors which would allow him to say his "woe" without dishonour.'

What dazzles and thrills throughout the thirty-year span of Imlah's work is his inventiveness, the sense of a mind pondering and producing at any turn something wholly unexpected, yet gleaming with its own unassailable rightness. A monologue by an aborted foetus, a 'Drinking Race' that becomes a descent into hell, an elegy for a rugby squad wiped out in the trenches, a journalist's visit to Lord Rosebery in his old age: there could hardly be a more varied list of subjects, yet each of the poems he made from them bears the stamp of his extraordinary ironic intelligence and truth to feeling. There was nothing he couldn't do, and might not have gone on to do for a rightful thirty years more. His early death was an incalculable loss to poetry.

Alan Hollinghurst

from BIRTHMARKS (1988)

Tusking

In Africa once
A herd of Harrow
Elephants strayed
Far from their bunks;
Leather, they laid
Their costly trunks
And ears of felt
Down on the Veldt.

All forgot
The creep of dusk;
A moonbeam stole
Along each tusk:
Snores and sighs.
Oh, foolish boys!
The English elephant
Never lies!

∼

In the night-time, lithe
Shadows with little
Glinting teeth
Whisked tusks away;
Drew through the dark
Branches of ivory,
Made a great hue
On their rapid run.

Hunters, at home
They curl up the bare
Soles of their feet
With piano-pleasure;
Sammy plays
A massacre song
With the notes wrong
On Massa's baby.

~

Out in the bush
Is silence now:
Savannah seas
Have islands now,
Smelly land-masses,
Bloody, cold,
Disfigured places
With fly-blown faces;

And each of us rests
After his fashion:
Elephant, English,
Butcher, Bushman;
Now only the herding
Boy in a singlet
Worries his goat
With a peaceful prod.

~

But if, one night
As you stroll the verandah
Observing with wonder
The place of the white
Stars in the universe,
Brilliant, and clear,
Sipping your whisky
And pissed with fear

You happen to hear
Over the tinkle
Of ice and Schubert
A sawing – a drilling –
The bellow and trump
Of a vast pain –
Pity the hulks!
Play it again!

Abortion

I woke the Monday after, feeling shabby
In a ship's bed, cramped in the head with the sense
That falls in private on forgetfulness
Of parties, that of someone's shame at me;

But waiting, I began to guess, would lick me
Properly into shape. Uncurled at noon
As dry as a Dead Sea Scroll, I rose and wobbled
Blank about the cabin like a reclaimed monster

Learning to eat; and through a glassy disk
Saw even passage, sun, unpoisoning sea,
And heard the call of sea-birds hosting me
To port, and hatched an eagerness for dusk

And drink, and company. And though I dozed again,
The clock had just snored twice without alarm
When (and I thought I was dreaming) a chink
Of cups began, like washing-up:

Then with only that warning the plates
Shook on my shelves which collapsed and smashed them,
And in the immediate stillness I felt as though someone
Was sitting behind me with news of disaster.

~

Have you ever heard a noise that you think
Is unearthly (especially when you're half asleep)
But when you get it into focus it's only
Them snoring, or your neighbour revving up?

Well that's how this whirring began,
Like something familiar mistaken, becoming
As I struggled to call it a pump or the cistern
Neither, nothing else, and very loud,

Till sailors' boasts fell silent in the spray.
When we took the first buffet I dropped
My pointless jacket and almost at once
I was doubled-up in air but couldn't breathe,

And dizzy I saw an experiment
With magnets, me the broken one,
A horseshoe facing down,
Sucked up. I passed clean out

And was lucky to survive; the boat
Melted in blood, but I stiffened safely,
A rabbit's foot, gristly
In someone's cabinet.

Clio's

Am I to be blamed for the state of it now? – Surely not –
Her poor wee fractured soul that I loved for its lightness and
    left?
Now she rings up pathetically, not to make claims of me,
Only to be in her wild way solicitous:
'Do you know of a restaurant called *Clio's* – or something
    like that –
At number *forty-three* in its road or street, – and the owner
Is beautiful, rich and Italian – you see, I dreamt of it,
And I can't relax without telling you never to go there,
Divining, somehow, that for you the place is *danger* –'

(But I dine at Clio's every night, poor lamb.)

Goldilocks

This is a story about the possession of beds.
It begins at the foot of a staircase in Oxford, one midnight,
When (since my flat in the suburbs of London entailed
A fiancée whose claims I did not have the nerve to evict)

I found myself grateful for climbing alone on a spiral
To sleep I could call with assurance exclusively mine,
For there was the name on the oak that the Lodge had assigned
Till the morning to me (how everything tends to its place!)

And flushed with the pleasing (if not unexpected) success
Of the paper on 'Systems of Adult-to-Infant Regression'
With which the Young Fireball had earlier baffled his betters
At the Annual Excuse for Genetics to let down its ringlets,

I'd just sniggered slightly (pushing the unlocked door
Of the room where I thought there was nothing of mine to protect)
To observe that my theory, so impudent in its address
To the Masters of Foetal Design and their perfect disciples,

Was rubbish – and leant to unfasten the window a notch, –
When I suddenly grasped with aversion before I could see it
The fact that the bed in the corner directly behind me
Had somebody in it. A little ginger chap,

Of the sort anthropologists group in the genus of *tramp*,
Was swaddled, as though with an eye to the state of the sheets,
With half of his horrible self in the pouch of the bedspread
And half (both his raggled and poisonous trouser-legs) out;

Whose snore, like the rattle of bronchial stones in a bucket,
Resounded the length and the depth and the breadth of the
    problem

Of how to establish in safety a climate conducive
To kicking him out – till at last I could suffer no longer

The sight of his bundle of curls on my pillow, the proof
That even the worst of us look in our sleep like the angels
Except for a few. I closed to within a yard
And woke him, with a curt hurrahing sound.

And he reared in horror, like somebody late for work
Or a debutante subtly apprised of a welcome outstayed,
To demand (not of me, but more of the dreary familiar
Who exercised in its different styles the world's

Habit of persecution, and prodded him now)
Phit time is it? – so you'd think that it made any difference –
So you'd think after all that the berth had a rota attached
And Ginger was wise to some cynical act of encroachment;

But when, with a plausible echo of fatherly firmness,
I answered, 'It's bedtime' – he popped out and stood in a shiver,
And the released smell of his timid existence swirled
Like bracing coffee between our dissimilar stances.

Was there a dim recollection of tenement stairways
And jam and the Rangers possessed him, and sounded a moment
In creaks of remorse? 'Ah'm sorry, son – Ah couldnae tell
They'd hae a wee boy sleepin here – ye know?'

(And I saw what a file of degradations queued
In his brown past, to explain how Jocky there
Could make me out to be innocent and wee:
As if to be wee was not to be dying of drink;

As if to be innocent meant that you still belonged
Where beds were made for one in particular.)
Still, the lifespan of sociable feelings is shortest of all
In the breast of the migrant Clydesider; and soon he relapsed

Into patterns of favourite self-pitying sentiments. 'Son –
Ah'm warse than – Ah cannae, ye know? Ah'm off tae ma
   dandy!
Ah've done a wee josie – aye, wheesh! – it's warse what Ah'm
   gettin –
Aye – warse!' And again the appeal to heredity – 'Son.'

(In the course of his speech, the impostor had gradually settled
Back on the bed, and extended as visual aids
His knocked-about knuckles; tattooed with indelible foresight
On one set of these was the purple imperative SAVE.)

Now I'm keen for us all to be just as much worse as we want,
In our own time and space – but not, after midnight, in my bed;
And to keep his inertia at bay, I went for the parasite,
Scuttling him off with a shout and the push of a boot

That reminded his ribs I suppose of a Maryhill barman's,
Until I had driven him out of the door and his cough
Could be heard to deteriorate under a clock in the landing.
(Och, if he'd known *I* was Scottish! Then I'd have got it.)

 ∾

But of course he came back in the night, when I dreamed I was
   coughing
And he stood by the door in the composite guise of a woman –
A mother, a doting landlady, a shadowy wife –
Sleepless as always, relieved nonetheless to have found me,

Or half-relieved – given what I had become;
Saying – 'It's just from the coughing and so on I wondered
If maybe a tramp had got into your bedroom' – and then,
Disappointedly: 'Couldn't you spare a wee thought for your dad?'

(I thought I was dreaming again on the train in the morning
To hear at my shoulder, before I had properly settled,

'Excuse me – is this seat taken?' spastically spoken;
But it wasn't our friend that I humoured through Didcot,
    and Reading,

No, but an anoracked spotter of diesels from Sheffield
Whose mind was apparently out in the sidings at Crewe:
Only one more in a world of unwanted connexions,
Who waved like a child when I fled for the toilet at Ealing.)

        ～

This is my gloss on the story of Goldilocks. Note:
It uncovers a naked and difficult thought about beds,
Namely, that seldom again will there ever be one
With only you in it; take that however you will.

Secrets

Where no one flushed the grass
A six-hit from the cricket,
We dealt in shallow sighs
Till hush! – she let her dress
Unbutton to the locket
And parted secrecies.

That evening, after hours,
The drink had drawn me close
To a team-mate, on a bench,
So I thought her secret ours;
And when a lull arose
I told it, for attention.

Unfit to be out naked
It lingered in the air
Like the fall of a far wicket;
But when at last he took it
With a snigger, and a glare,
And a hand across his pocket

The word was up and gone.
It spread like danger, blown
From ear to burning ear
Across a field of corn;
And though I sprinted home
I later sought repair

(As every charring shadow
Creeps to quench its source)
And found renewed at dawn
A cricket pitch – a meadow –
And the patch of flattened grass
A black dog squatted on.

Lee Ho Fook's

What brought the Chinaman down to the building-site? Ah, it
    was Fate;
And Fate in the scaffolding kicked from its cradle the vat,
Thirty foot over his dithering head, of boiling and thunderous
    tea.
Who was on hand, though, to rush from his post and manhan-
    dle the fellow
(Then of a frightened, diminutive, immigrant state of fragility)
Into a sheltering barrow, the moment the day's brew exploded
Exactly where seconds before he'd been staring and dreaming
    of mountains
And seagulls and sails in the harbour? Charlie Wood.

The building-site is buildings now, the Cannon Street Office
Of the Hong Kong and Cantonese Bank – and all would be
    buried beneath
Were it not for the Chinaman's blur of cross-cultural gratitude:
'You have saved my life. The least I can do in return
Is to ask you to dine as my guest in my fabulous restaurant
Whenever you will.' 'Well thanks very much,' says Charlie –
'I might take you up on that offer.' – Back to the grit and the
    grind;
Thinking, though, *Tell you what, Charlie Boy, could be a bit of
a bonus!*

Indeed, while the mind of this builder was normally dark,
And dripping with flesh, and unwholesome, infested, and
    spotty, a shaft
Of purest sunshine scored suddenly over the tracks as he
    pondered his luck;
And a sluice and an avalanche opened of rice and prawns like
    the coins in *The Golden Shot*

Churning and pouring forever and all of it aimed at his lap;
Which drew him away from the mix of cement he was feeding
And up in a daze to the Works hut, and on through a dozen or
    more
Inscrutable *Yellow Pages* – well, it would take him a couple of
    tea-breaks . . .

Years pass. And the tiny impulse of distaste Lee had felt
At his saviour's first beaming appearance and chirpy request for
    a knife and fork
Has swollen; of late it resembles a sort of unsociable illness
That has to be kept in check by a sidling withdrawal to the
    stairs
Whenever his own lucky star, with its multiple coatings of
    yesterday's earth,
Comes rollicking in for the freebies – as often as three times a
    week.
(Something is fouling the lock in the door to his dream of new
    premises;
Something as fixed as the bambooey bulge in Charlie Wood's
    cheek.)

So Charlie is left to chew over the Chinaman's lapses of honour
And nibble at rightful reprisals: *When his highness emerges at
    last*
To slide me as ever the ready-paid bill on a saucer
(Disguising by this, he supposes, his part of the bargain)
What if I dashed this half-cup of their pissy tea at him –
Out of the blue, to remind him why Woodsy is here?
*– Or when they've been keeping me waiting an hour for the
    soup, to come out with it –*
Oy, son, I had you in a barrow once – *instead of my usual?*

Visiting St Anthony

'*St Anthony's Bunker*, fifty miles by jeep;
Not often touristed, and very cheap;
The humble desert home of ANTHONY,
Oldest of human beings, and a saint.'

I don't remember what I half-expected
When I picked that xeroxed advert from the rest
And made my booking, to the mild surprise
Of the agent, in his shuttered, dingy room;

Long tracts of beard, perhaps, on a bony
Story-teller; or skin to prod, with a pig
Fast at one ankle; but I don't remember.
We came upon it after hours of sand.

'Mister,' the guide implored, the truck slowing,
'The saint is at his books . . .' I smelt a rat;
And sure enough, we dwindled to a stop
At what he called 'respectful' yards away

From terror, or complaint, before a sign
Whose motto's paint dribbled sarcastically:
AS THE FISH REMOVED FROM WATER SLOWLY DIES
SO DOES THE MONK WHO WANDERS FROM HIS CELL

– What 'cell'? – What pilgrim dared they hope to fool
By the bivouac of planks that Tuesday's hands
Had scrambled up to scarcely overlook
Miles of a wasted journey? Or plonked on top,

What chance that the poor beggar bound to a stool
With half a hymnal stuffed between his knees
Couldn't be dead? It wasn't cloth, but wire
That kept him blindfold, and his skull intact,

And nothing surgical that plugged the holes
Where saints have eyes. I measured up the fraud:
They'd raked this load of maggots from his thin
Pittance of rest, for my few quid – Arabs!

So much the worse my second shock. I saw
The skull, beneath its ragged hood of flesh,
Bend, like a monk's white face, as if to read;
And when, at once, it buckled and recoiled

There came a foul noise, like the waking cry
Of dogs behind the oil-drums of his door
And that was all; the pages fluttered over
Like profit counted; and the guide resumed.

'The chain leads to the Saint's devoted PIG,
Which is a thing like Mary's little lamb
Or the love of God for every hopeless man,
Whose patience is so gross, it will survive

Although the pig is very old, for a pig –
Even as old as Master Anthony.'
But there was no pig to be seen, anywhere,
Of any age, unless that hump of flies –

And I don't suppose we'd parked for a minute, before
I motioned to the guide to turn for town;
Who thought me scared, no doubt, but knew the tomb,
And was himself no chicken, as he said.

from The Counties of England

Bedfordshire

A class of ambitious young toe-rags has failed *en bloc*
To come up with a slogan that captures their county of Beds.
Each is condemned to drive off in his GT to fritter
A reasonable income on lager in Dunstable winebars.
Meanwhile, the cleaner is sifting their mound of rejections
And nodding at every half-hearted depiction of Eden . . .

Berkshire

Any day now we'll be watching the battle of Berkshire,
To be fought on boats at a picturesque turn in the water
Between (in the red trunks) thirty-six bargees from Reading
And a shimmering squadron of angels descending from Cookham.
Only the late Stanley Spencer can picture the outcome;
Only the late Stanley Spencer can ransom the angels.

Herefordshire

Another breakdown has amazed the Scoutcamp.
What can't they cope with? Bikers in the square?
Dragonflies buzzing their blue canoes, or the closeness
Of black-and-white cattle as big as Ledbury houses?
Is it the secret of beer? Or is it the arrogant
Daughters of Kilpeck, flaunting their better childhood?

Leicestershire

Leicestershire gentlemen like to be seen
Down the wrong end of a horn or a sporting gun.
The wrecked complexion blaring at the rabbit
And the notorious Grace Road bark at an Indian batting
Are products of the same inverted nightmare –
A fox on horseback riding down fat pigs.

Northamptonshire

Retrieved from the ash of a collapsed loft in Daventry
The Complete History of the County of Northamptonshire
Whose text and the numerous inserts have melted together.
For instance: 'A Family Cobbler the Choice of a Prince'
Is the heading of one of the later, industrial chapters
And 'Shoeing Britannia's March Through the Centuries' –
     that was an ad.

Oxfordshire

1943: working in secret, assured
That the pact preserving the beauties of Oxford and Dresden
Would be bombed flat, – Lord Cowley and others project
A magnificent *Oxford Rebuilt* on a radial pattern
With circular colleges, ring roads, and orbital cemeteries . . .
(Nuffield to Churchill: We've got the phoenix – now you
     deliver the ashes . . .)

Rutland

Here it was always a summer evening. An obsolete
Male population of steeplejacks trail, through the Uppingham
    streets
And the alleys of Oakham, traditional portions of woodsmoke
Homewards to wives in their cottages dreaming as ever of
    cheeses;
While over the toby-jug factory, over the orchard of cherries
Creeps the abolishing shadow of wicked Squire Locust of Gall.

Somerset

The musical birds who give tune to the joys of the county
Have chosen today to forsake their particular perches
Of honey and ivy at Crewkerne, and Wookey, and Mells,
And empty the comfortable echoing glades of the Quantocks
To sit with the stillness of leaves in the afternoon shadow
Of Taunton's twin towers: big Botham and Richards.

Quasimodo Says Goodnight

To think that you could go to sleep in a bed
That I made up, with hair like that unbound
On a shirt I wore last week! I should be sorry,
Esmeralda, should I? I am wicked
Sneaking back to watch you sleeping – am I?
For you cannot as you surely would express
Our difference in painful gesture; cannot
Wince, or feel for the wall, or quickly thank me
For my beans or let that pity fly
Sidelong; but now encircled by my tread
You suffer each unseen approach in silence
Or a sigh, and fumbling trespass fails because
While you pretend this deafness I can call you
Esmeralda, and you cannot think me
Beast; because I want you, and I should not.

And yet come closer; look, your mouth is open
Where a little purse of air blows in and out
And in and out; and in the mild adventure
Of a dream you cannot scale the height
To which these hands have hauled your daily fear:
Above, ten yards of tower; beyond, thin air;
Below, a wink of bonfire, memories
Of spite as faint as drowning, pale as water.
And neither does your shuttered sense admit
That you must eat my meals; that whosoever
You consider beautiful seems not
To come, though I do not mean he will not, nor
To stop him; or that I am stooping closer,
And could love you as I pleased while you
Could only hate more closely than you do.

I'd know by touching whether you were cold;
But you'll forgive me that I'm not allowed
To have a fire inside, not if the walls
Were stacked with frozen saints or riddled with devils.
The Deacon says unholy fires will break
The spell that makes the building everlasting;
This is not true he says when priests make fires
Either for light or to extinguish witches.
May I pull this blanket up? there's a gap,
You see, the cold will muscle in
And wake you up; your back is half-uncovered.

How accidental human beauty seems!
Imagine God's great metalworks, with scores
Of anxious pigmies running up and down
The length of complicated moulds with rods
And steamed-up rules and paints all day, who see
That of the flowers tinkling from the mint
Not one is blotched or crooked. Somewhere else
More hazy floats a chapel with a cage,
Where a pair of dozy journeymen play marbles
With mounds of hopeless heads: one afternoon
Exchanging nods and leers, they turn a lock
And giggling climb a circle like a stair,
And enter where they think they shouldn't, watched,
And think they steal; but from the holy pouch
Unspotted by the thief that bore it out
Is drawn and spun a careless miracle
To tease us. Beauty waits, and knows its hour,
And falls in questions: why, for one, when somebody
Great has died and I've been swinging hell
For leather on the bells, and now I've stopped
And I'm sprawled drunk on my lofty beams does the song

Of hooded boys creep up in draughts and breezes,
Chill me, and I cry, and no one knows?
Or when I saw your naked back just now,
Because in the end I had to, just at the simple
Form of it, why did I shudder and see flame?
Could you, who did it, tell me? Could the Deacon?

If we were of one element, say beauty –
Look how my fancy shuffles from the shadow,
Free of its shame, but shy to be an act,
To rouse you with a face, and not a plate,
And greet you with a smile, and get a smile;
To ease you from the crusty bedding inch
By dazzling inch, by unimagined inch;
To throw the trapdoor on new feats of air
And raise enormous fires, and laugh down loud
At crumbling roofs and chalky-haired forbidders,
And when we perished in my clasp we'd stay
And go like stone together, and be thought stone
By the Deacon, and he'd overpay the Mason,
And a new boy would toll the morning bell, –
But my beauty is all in dreams; and now you stir,
Poor angel; you have slept with me; thank you.

Cockney

How heightened the taste! – of champagne at the piano; of
  little side-kisses to tickle the fancy
At the party to mark our sarcastic account of the overblown
  Mass of the Masses by Finzi
(An aristocrat who betrayed what he stood for and set up in
  Bow with his matchgirl fiancée);

Moreover, the skit I had chosen to grace the occasion ('*My
  Way* – in the Setting for Tuba by Mahler')
Had even the Previns in generous stitches (it seemed an
  acceptable social *milieu*
If only because it was something like six million light years
  away from the planet of Millwall)

When the buffet arrived; and as we applauded the *crudités*
  carved into miniature flats and sharps
There crept into mind for a desperate moment the ghost of
  me mum shuffling back from the shops
With a Saturday treat – 'Look! We got sausages, beans, an'
  chips!'

So I mentally told her to stuff it, and turned, with a shivering
  reflex of anger
To harangue a superior brace of brunettes for their preference
  of Verdi to Wagner;
But again she appeared at the door, with the salt and the
  sacred vinegar

And I was reclaimed. 'You!' she demanded, 'You who last
  month in the Seychelles
Took drinks with a Marquess, and studded the spine of
  Lucinda with seashells –

You are the same little boy that I sent out in winter with
    Cockney inscribed on your satchel!'

And as she dispersed, one or two of my neighbours were squint-
    ing at me as you do a bad odour,
And even my friendly advances were met by a flurry of coughs
    and a mutter of *Oh, dear* –
For try as I might I just couldn't assemble the sounds that
    came out in a delicate order:

ALL ROYT MOY SAHN! HA'S YOR FARVAH?
LEN YOU TEN NOWTS? – CALL IT A FOIVAH!
TRAVELLED IN TEE-ASCANY? - DO ME A *FIVAH*!

And worse was to follow. For over this bleak ostinato of base-
    born vowels
I detected the faraway strains of a disco remix of *The Dance
    of the Seven Veils*
And felt the lads egging me on to enact what a tug at the
    Seventh reveals –

Yes, down came the pants of old Rotherhithe's rugged
    Salomé,
And pointing it straight at the toff who was leading the charge
    to assail me
Out of my shirtfront I prodded two-thirds of a purple salami . . .

    ∾

Sometimes, there's a song in my head as I sit down at tea, and I
    know what the tune is
But can't catch the words. And when I get tired of the humming,
    it's off down to Terry's, or Tony's,
A couple of pints, then across to the club till it closes, for
    snooker with Pakistanis.

Silver

Silver in block or chain
Will not sustain
   The nameless slaves
   Who row it through the waves

As long as the old, crude
Hallmark tattooed
   On every chest
   Proclaims them second-best.

Wherever the ship may steer
They face the rear;
   What lies in store
   Is untransmuted ore.

Breaking into the bungalow, we found
His last meal full of maggots on the cooker,
Four hundred and forty-six pounds in pound notes
In various vases and drawers,
And a bowls cup from the Fifties, silvery-brown,
By the tin of Duraglit –
He had been polishing it.

Mountains

O the mind, mind has mountains . . .
   – HOPKINS

Snowdonian

At the start of our climbing career
Each had his flask, his blue kagul
And a uniform will to be first
In the sprint to the peak;
Nobody thought it was steep
Or fell far out of step.

So, back at the gabled hostel,
There were coffee and biscuits, a perfect
Unnecessary roll-call,
Viollet, *Wavering*,
White, *Wood*,
And no weak link exposed;

Though on the downward scree
Slipping and dying in jest
Twyford (2Y) had spotted a single
Classic sure-foot, bearded goat
Lost to the herd, broken-backed
Among heathery boulders.

Alpine

Stranded at base
When the four had gone
To grow for a gown
Frost's blue fur,

On my mind's reel
I seemed to follow
Their blurrying through
The storm's crackle

Till, wavering,
White against white,
They shivered off the screen
Like watermarks . . .

Now in the sun
Twisting blue
Daisies across
Finger and thumb,

I think I hear one
Of the frayed chain
Or the ghost of one
Baring bad gifts:

'Here are my hands'
(I think I see them)
'Violet and white
And hard as wood.'

Himalayan

Concern about our provisions was to cost us many sleepless nights
  – SIR JOHN HUNT

Roof of the world; rumble of avalanche; something attacking
The splintering walls of our matchstick lodge with a vengeance;
And all I could glimpse from the sleeping bag (face to the floor-
    boards'
Powdery glass) was a snowdrift of beans, and a Nescafé label, –
These were the last of our rations exploding about us!

(And it struck me again, in the hail from a cereal packet,
As when the kitchen in Ballater crackled with fire
From a fault in the toaster, the everyday nature of danger;
When even our comforts can turn, and our breakfast itself
Come in volleys against us.) And then he was there: there, at
    the door –

There, with his featureless face at a gap in the ceiling –
Abominable, the Monster of the Slope,
Furry with frost, in the guise of a ghastly storeman:
'Get off my mountain. Get off my world.'
– Slapping huge coffee-jars into our lodge.

Polar

Sometimes all Nature seems for us, sometimes against
    – EDWARD WHYMPER

. . . For perhaps twenty minutes we stood petrified in the darkness as an innumerable dense flock of penguins swept over us, blotting out the sun and the sky, all inclined upwards as though in an aerial charge at the summit . . .

. . . The final push has been postponed again, in the wake of a horrid discovery. After good progress earlier this morning, we had slowed somewhat by noon when Hislop, who was leading, let out a series of screams, like a man who has found his skin covered with unexpected creatures. I crabbed as quickly as possible to his assistance, and though I could not understand him at first, he managed to convey by gestures that he had scraped his boot with a pick, and found *beaks*. I checked my own footing, and examined the lines of a ridge above, where the coating of blackish ice petered out like slush; and in a moment it became unpleasantly clear to me that we had been climbing in the mist on a sort of frosted mud made of penguins, for miles and miles.

. . . Morphine! and monstrous dreams . . . All nature for us or against us. I have no pictures of that bed of penguins.

?

Because it isn't there . . . I slipped and fell
A thousand feet; woke with my boots on

And the camp doctor's hand weighing my wrist
As he said gently, son, your nerve has gone.

Birthmark

On my decline, a millipede
Helped me to keep count;
For every time I slipped a foot
Farther down the mountain

She'd leave a tiny, cast-off limb
Of crimson on my cheek
As if to say –
You're hurting us both, Mick . . .

I saw in this gradual sacrifice
No end of merriment:
A broken vein or two; hardly
Memento mori.

This thousandth morning after, though
(Or thousand-and-first)
I miss her, and a bedside mirror
Bellows the worst –

A big, new, bilberry birthmark, stamped
From ear to livid ear,
Her whole body of blood's
Untimely smear.

She must have found, shaking her sock
For warnings, that the hoard was spent,
And had to stain me with her death
To show what she meant:

That it's as bad to fall astray
As to start from the wrong place.
Now I have earned the purple face.
It won't go away.

The Drinking Race

The Irish Team

Lowly, degraded things: *Guinness* with no head;
Yeats's Father at O'Donoghue's, shouting his usual joke:
'This Land of Saints' (ignored by the usual crowd)
'– Of plastered Saints'; his flies greatly undone.
Maud Gonne in need of help, lungeing between the tables,
Her great grey skirt hoiked up, abused by all;
Augusta Gregory huddling from scorpions under a Formica
    table,
And scaring the scorpions; *Lionel Johnson* challenging God:
'I told Him that nightly from six to eleven I perch on this
    barstool –
Haha!' – and over he goes; and *Yeats* in the corner, combing
    the heads
And the tables for bits of potato to turn into slabs of marble
In poems where his friends are made to look better than
    everyone else's,
Calls them 'Olympians'. (All's changed, etc.)

Brawl in Co. Kerry

I was in the bar at Castlemaine with June
Until, at half past ten, a word fell wrong
Between O'Leary and the little man
Who whacked glass on O'Leary's leaning head

And launched the brawl. I've memorised the barman
Lost in a boxing stance behind his bar,
And wheeling arms, and windmill sprays of stout; –
A moment's lull; then a surge, and bundling June

Flat to the bench, and the sudden pointed eyes
Under the cap across the room of the drunk
Who because we looked afraid, or young, or British
Or sober, and seemed to judge, or just because,

Threw from a sitting position his glass at us
Which struck my fending arm. Above us now
O'Leary sad from battle, howling and shaking
Blood from his shaggy head like a soaked retriever.

∼

'Jesus,' Bernard groans, '– you should have thrown
Your own glass back at that bastard.' But instead
When a gap had appeared to the door we'd gone for it
And hurried stooping up the stony hill

With my split elbow. 'Look,' I teased, 'this white
Stripe is the tendon' (meant to make her squeal);
But though she shivered like a windy day
Her face was weird with rage. She and the moon

Blinked at each other through the mottled speed
Of fugitive clouds; and from the walled-up fields
There came a sound like a host's embarrassed cough,
The formal tick tick of the tongueless cricket.

Starter's Orders

These warless days
Men without women
Thirst for the means
To waste themselves;

It's in the blood.
Their fathers worked
And Grandad breasted
A barbed tape;

But now where the girls
Are sick of courage
Men without hope
Of a job, or a bayonet,

Muster like champions
Under a canopy,
Over a barrel,
Primed for the slaughter;

Fit to pursue
Illness, dishonour,
And sponsored to boot.
Gentlemen, swallow!

Strange Meeting

As I walked down towards the Drinking Race
I overtook one combatant, whose legs
Wandered abandoned under a wet face
Rubbed ruby-red by life's abrasive dregs.

He'd jumped the gun over the rest of them
And looked a certain finalist, when he slowed
To clear his throat of the obstructive phlegm
And hailed me, as I tried to cross the road.

'You coward! You! Come here!' (He took a draught
And what he drank came straight back through his nose)
'Don't you appreciate the drinker's craft?
Why won't you stop and sup with us old pros?'

When I declined, he straightened for a spell
On his best leg, and spat from this strange stance
Like a heron proud of its own repulsive smell
Or furious at a biped's arrogance:

'With better luck, I'd catch you in a fight
Or institutional combat at the bars,
And you wouldn't know if it was day or night
For the ringing in your ears, and the seeing stars;

But meantime – that's unless you'd care to part
With twenty pence?' (I smirked) '– Meantime' (his face
Drew far too close) 'You have an evening's start,
And meet me downstairs at the Drinking Race!'

Silver Medals

Here on the last lap of the Marathon
A cruel invisible wall or wire or moat
Has baulked the Bavarian champion, and he lies
Unconscious, fifty yards from the champagne . . .

– Cut to his fiancée, winner at sixteen
Of the High Jump gold for girls at the Munich Games
(Where twelve Israeli athletes came to grief)
And also here – how did she read his fall?

But hold the replay – something's wrong; she gags;
She drapes his tracksuit over a monitor;
She sobs, at last, 'You see, –' (there at the vault
Someone's arching back) '– I know he died –'

(And for that spasm, we see a field full of him
Slaughtered in earnest: village Olympians,
Their spoons flung out to catch the spilling eggs)
'– Like in his last race, up at Helsinki.'

And again we're glad of silver medals; glad
Of easy resurrections, and returns
From the darkest hangovers; happy to share
The lie that doing your best is all that counts;

To know that the lame, the lost, the left-behind,
Even the least significant dead German,
Stumble about in the kit that Glory wears
And have their minute on the uncut tape;

That we ourselves will soon be driving home,
At dusk, along familiar chestnut roads,
To join the reel of people we've come to trust
To take no notice – only a day more failing;

That the tall West German girl was using 'died'
In the milder, athletic sense, and only meant
Her friend (*not* an Immortal of the Track)
Had finished with less pep than he'd have liked.

Hall of Fame

It seemed that from the beer-tent I escaped
Down some profound depression, where they kept

Silent the damaged and the down-and-out.
A sergeant rang the bell for them to eat,

That being the hour appointed; but the failures
Who shuffled from the darkness on all fours

Had burned away their appetite for solids
And only a couple accepted watery salads

To sip at on their disinfected bunks.
These were the veterans of such bloody banquets
Eternal headaches hurt them, and still hurt;
'Hey soldier!' I called at one I seemed to hate

Who was sitting helpless in his vest and pants
Over a tray of flat insipid pints:

'Didn't I see you when you were so pissed
On the road here, that a mug of whisky passed

Straight back out of your nostrils as you drank?
Tell me, how did a soldier get that drunk?

And how did you fare later?' Out of luck
He shed his numbered shorts and made me look

At something that I wished I had not seen,
The ruined arse-hole, flapping, crudely sewn,

Through which he spoke: 'After the rout – I lost,
I think, or won – came either first or last –

'They bore me up, oblivious to my wound,
On eager shoulders; but before they could be warned,

With a loud noise, the crap larruped down my leg.
Now every Christmas I raise half a lager

To absent friends; and absent is the word,
For nobody loves me in the Drinking Ward

Or brings me chocolates or forget-me-nots . . .'
So moaning he withdrew; the last three notes

Blew like reveille from their fading source.

The Zoologist's Bath

> 'Among the more eccentric exponents of evolutionary theory . . .
> [was] . . . Arthur William Woolmer (1833–80). His most contro-
> versial thesis, detailed in the posthumous *Decline of the Mammal*,
> that land species, having descended from sea-going forms, would
> strive to return to their original element, won few adherents . . .
> His "crowning race" would have been the merman.'
>   – T. A. PAISH, *The Sciences in the Victorian Age*, 1949, p.139

I

It happened as I settled after Partridge came
With the tea and my petit-point, which she'd cleverly found,
So that I was arranged with all the things I would need
For an ordinary week-day evening's entertainment;
And Arthur had gone up to take his bath.
How did I know? The noise was not excessive,
And years should have got me used to the once queer
Begrudging scrape of the staircase door, and yet –
Like a clock that ticks its way through a steady childhood,
And then, as the family sit by the fire in all
The assurance of what they are known to enjoy, stops,
And frightens them more than the dark or a wild man –
The door and the business of whispers now, when the house
Should prefer to be quiet, had me out of my rug in a second.
Partridge was biting her pinny, and the new man bossy,
Insisting 'I shouldn't go up, miss' – my own brother,
He seemed to be saying, would want to avoid needing me.
I was up the flickering stairs in a moment and running
Beyond the awakening tentacles and startling teeth
Of the landing gallery and into his bubbling chamber
Where such was my rush and conviction of aid that I
Saw him before I could hope to avert my sight.

[42]

2

The same thing happens every time I bathe;
Something about the tumble of the water
On my blunted toes, or the sense of home I get
Watching the slow waving of my little hairs
Like reeds above a monster, sets me off.
I know it's not the popular idea
Of scientific method – getting wet –
But neither's raking up what the wind brought down
For Mrs Newton; neither's making tea
Somewhere in Scotland. Think of Syracuse,
Whose greatest minds, as Gelon's *Chronicle*
Of Ancient Sicily records, would rise
Each dawn, and gather in a school, and home
Like clever lemmings on their natal club,
The civic lavatory. ('Laboratories'
Evolved in ageing Caesar's deaf left ear
When ships brought him; and since his sad mistake
We've toiled in smelly rooms for little drops
Of stuff that's on tap everywhere – the truth.)
But Syracuse! I see their happy wise,
Each in his lukewarm tank and smirking down
At something raving in the square below –
Hot-blooded Archimedes doing physics –
Now they duck under with a nod, and will bask
Knowingly till sunset. When I feel
My bottom buoyed, and start to think of fish,
I am at one with them; and furthermore
As Catherine says it keeps me pretty clean.

Well, what I see at first is a tap or tube
Like that big loopy rectum the koala hides,
And out of it streaming a stuff like creamy pupae,

Thick with little eyes, and full of fins,
Splashing into the water and diffusing.
This generates a wonderful parade
Of landed species bearing liquid children,
Or frankly, shitting fish. I'll see a pheasant
Issue unshelled spawn, a cow discharge
Its mackerel in pats, a vivid worm
Crack as the pike slides out. And suddenly
Hypotheses will rocket round my skull
Like starfish rolled by gulls across the sky;
Are not the night secretions of the tern,
For instance, like an oily saw-dust, sign
Of the discreet development of gills?

Surely the Hebrew Sages knew about it –
What happened to the fish in Noah's Flood?
Had they no sin to choke for, that the world
Became what might be called their oyster? Did two
Of each variety (and Holder counts
Five hundred thousand submarine divisions)
Angle themselves? Did Noah's little boy
Devise, one drizzly breakfast while his dad
Was lecturing the lions and the dodos,
A warm aquarium to sleep a million?
He didn't. Germans have mapped the Bible's truth
Meandering out of Science into Symbol;
How could you justify a family
Of *eight* to countless legions of mere pairs?
We must assume that only two were human,
Including, I imagine, *Shem*. Discount
The nagging *Wife*, a medieval shrew;
And *Ham*, the pig that none of them could eat;
Sore in the seed of the drowsy baby hummed

The order *Iaphetoptera* (wood-wasps);
And the paragon, Old Noah, was a whale.
Try proving it? You're in the Deluge, right,
And someone says, I'll bet you drown, you're wicked;
What would you splash to, an ancient ape with a hammer
Or a hulk with a mouth the size of Crystal Palace?
Of course you would. Remember when we read
The Other Testament that its skull-capped bards
Had motives of their own, religious ones;
No journalist wrote Genesis; no Jew
Would think of other species. Noah's ark
Was Noah, the chosen mammal. Evidence?
The eye-witness account appears in *Jonah*,
Those ghosted memoirs of the bashful Shem.
(Nor can we swallow in the modern age
The biblical account of what took place
At the Red Sea; it occurs to me that Moses
Was vestigially amphibious; his tribe,
Adaptable; the Egyptians, stony lizards.)

But these are only signs; and did our God
When feastless we moaned through Sinai, when our nets
Strayed loose on Galilee, torment our sense
With whispers of manna, bulging basketfuls
Of shadow? Nor shall our appetite for fact
Go belly-aching; we have tongued the flesh,
Abused it, called it man, and hooked it up
For the sharp winds and the centuries to hurt,
Till eating it at last we give it names
Like 'bread' if we are Sunday Methodists
Or 'fish' if Friday Catholics, who stand
Like bullies on the hilltop, nearer God.
Nor in the days of His ministry was Christ

Ever unsilver, ever coarse with hair
Or long in the open air. Two points should seal it;
First, did He walk on water? Did He need to?
And secondly, what emblem did they choose,
His persecuted followers, and why?
And does not man aspire to that? Do I?
I wrinkle, underwater, in ten minutes.
Before the hour, I shall have a fin.

from THE LOST LEADER (2008)

Muck

(AD)

Hey, we were only semi-literate
ourselves: we meant to head for Mull, not
where the blessed Kevin miscarried us,
a rank bad place with no words at all.

It was about the year dot – before
MacBrayne and the broken ice; before
Colum and Camelot, whose annals skate
over our failed attempt on Muck –

when the call came (I didn't hear it)
to rid ourselves of the Ulster roof-
and-cake mentality, and work abroad.
So we did go, in wash-tub coracles,

and hauled ashore for an hour or so, on a
black upturned platter of rock, stained
with sea-lichen and scummy pools
of barge flies and crab water.

No trees, then. No welcoming men
or women either. But out on a spur's end
we spotted a sham temple – being a few
upright poles fashioned from driftwood, which

when we straggled over to them, seemed,
without a text or rune to vent their purpose,
to have their say in fish. ('That's one
of our symbols,' said Kevin, slowly.)

~

The first was crude, like holy rood,
a shark hung where the Christ might be.
The crossbeam of the second, wavy,
white and queasy, was split three times

by dolphins' leaps and falls; while each
of the mounting horizontals of the next,
carved with a rogue's dash or abandon,
was a fish-beam: the worst given the arc

of a catfish – though closer to, we saw
how this was worked from a lower jaw,
the bass jaw of an ox. These three might seem
the project of a class of kids; except

for the cunning which had placed the group
of crosses, if we call them crosses,
in silhouette, against the setting sun,
her *lux in embro*; or the paler moon.

The fourth was set apart. It wore
the red back half of a toy tractor, fixed
to the neck of a pole; and strapped to the spine,
a thermos, meant to last the afternoon . . .

– the cairn beneath it had been plugged, once,
with a plastic helmet – that was bleached by now
from orange to lime or yellow; and over the whole
was thrown a mongrel dress of fishnet and floats.

~

K saw a fifth, with his second sight,
and wasn't telling. Only, 'Back to the boats! –
It's no good, we brought the word of God
to those in hiding here, and they don't want it!'

(So we sounded in reply the child's note
of feigned frustration, masking the relief
our code forbids us to have felt, or
having felt, express.) Till as we sucked

our wicker boats and heels clear of their shingle,
he struck up from the front, bellowing out
Our Founder's Lesson, 'Study the Mountains' (strange
how the borrowed prose would fill him full of himself) –

'*Study the mountains; then when you fancy
that you know the mountains, you can learn the stars.*'
(Just then, Kevin, none of us rowing could
see past the grimed horizon of your neck;

and as the squall got up, you couldn't hear
half that we aimed in reply; until with the double
beating of salt and rain on our hands and face
we sank back in the bee-shape; kept at the oars.

But we will expect something to sustain us,
soon, beyond the Plough and the Sperrins.
In the meantime, here's to the gay goddess
Astarté – mother of false starts!)

The Prophecies

1 *Of the book which fell into the water-vessel*

ONE day, as he was staring into the hall-fire
with such sadness, that the serving brethren
redoubled their normal silence – he caught sight
in a corner of the youth Lugbe, from the clan Cummin,
reading a book, and suddenly said to him,
not in a threatening way, 'Take care, my son,
for it seems that the book you are reading is about
to fall into a vessel full of water.'

And so it proved: for when in time the boy
stood up to fetch a candle, he seemed to forget
the prophetic warning, and as he passed by
one of the saint's more senior men the book
slipped from under his arm, and lo! it was text-
down in the foot-bath, which was full of water.

2 *Similar, of the Thuringian inkhorn*

ONE day, when a shout went up on the far side
of the Sound of Hy, the saint, who had made for himself
an hour apart in his room, to meditate,
grew aware of the shout, and said, 'The man who is shouting
beyond the Sound is not of very sharp wit,
since when he comes knocking here today
for his food, or a spiritual lesson, he will surely
upset my Thuringian inkhorn, and spill the ink.'

This put his monks in a quandary, – whether
to bring the thing on, or to prevent it;
and some were busy, and some were standing still
the moment the shouter arrived: who in his haste
to embrace the saint, brushed the desk with a trailing
sleeve and we all had to write about it.

3 *Of the dead letter*

ONE day Baithene, his old attendant, asked him:
'Could you spare a learned brother to read the psalter
your servant has written, and correct it?' To which
the saint replied: 'Why give my staff the trouble?
I daresay that in this psalter of yours, there is not
one word or letter too many; on the other hand,
look again at the work, and you will find
that everywhere the vowel 'i' is omitted!'

Now when Baithene went back to the manuscript,
and checked it over, he found to his amazement
that in his absence some tick had gone over
his stuff and with a blue pencil scored out
every sentence in the first person, including
the entire intro and the acknowledgements.

4 *Of a future book*

Of course it got better, when he grew older
and sitting at supper was less apt to see
Judas in everyone's face at his shoulder:
'the wheels', as he put it, 'secure on the axle',
our wagon was 'fit to roam into the future'.

Thus, once, he emerged from a session, the dark
of his eyes rolled back from view – a trick he had –
and spoke of a small, black, impending book:

The Life of St Columba, Founder of Hy
by Adam something – many an abbot later –
in Penguin Classics, nineteen ninety-nine.
And now as he shared the vision he felt, he said,
a warm, delicious tingle and flush of the veins
as if he had been ravished by who knows whom.

I

Elderly, veiny, eccentric: our guide, running
a leak from his nose, with not enough coat

to keep out the flat rain or hail of Iona,
is 'taking the story on from Columba'.

For here, as our Lord's first millennium bumped
on its dark philological bottom or *nadir*,

they carried the freezing body of Fergus Mor,
crawled through the winter to give him grace;

Fergus, whose ancestral line or graveway
appears as a series of pock marks in the grass.

Is nothing sacred? Not the burial ground
of the ur-kings, the first Scots known by name?

'. . . And Fergus's son was Domangart MacFergus;
and he "begat" Comgall MacDomangart;

who in his turn begat – *aheugh!* – MacComgall,
begat Ferchar . . . begat Ainbcellach Mac

cheugh! Mac Ferchar, begat *aheugh!* Muiredach
Mac – heigh, ho – Eochaid the Venomous –

and thirty more I *could* name, but for this
caaatchoo! – down to your own John Smith. *Ahem.*'

Fergus of Galloway

(Fergus attempts to make off with the shield of Dunottar)

When Fergus drew his pathetic weapon,
The dragon froze, with her mouth open –
As if to say, *I'm petrified*;
That the doomed knight might peep inside
Her filthy width of flame and froth –
Then shut it, with a snap of wrath.

No man in such a pass would choose
To linger with all he had to lose:
None but Sir Fergus, who possessed
The stoutest heart in the South West.
So there he stayed, at the beast's whim,
Until she slapped her tail at him,

Which made him glad he'd grabbed the shield;
For though it cracked, it wouldn't yield,
And kept him – for the moment – sound.
But then he tried to stand his ground,
And found his boots were treading water,
And as he cartwheeled through Dunottar

He struck a wall with such a crack
His ribs were crushed against his back,
And all his senses so displaced
He thought he heard a burning taste.
The dragon, meanwhile, stopped and wept
At the cradleside where her shield had slept,

As if in a Highland melodrama.
Sir Fergus cursed through buggered armour.
His only solace where he lay,
That chevalier of Galloway,
Was joining, where he moaned and bled,
The ranks of the heroic dead.

For so much blood had spouted out
Of his wounds from the first blow of the bout
That when his eyes fell on the hue
Of the tunic he had put on blue,
He almost fainted in distress
At the ruined state of his warrior dress.

Instead, provoked by the red rag,
He sprang up, like a cornered stag,
And threw the weight of his wounded pride
At the tough scales of the lizard's hide –
Then slicing up at her peevish head,
Punctured the neck and dropped her dead.

Now, had you asked him to disown
His day's work, for the English throne
Or a long drink from our Saviour's Cup,
He would have told you to shut up,
So pleased was he to sniff the air
As Fergus of Galloway – Dragon-Slayer!

(from the French poem *Fergus*, c.1155)

Michael Scot

(1175–1232)

A fresco in the church of Santa Maria Novella
in Florence shows a friar urging repentance
on a crowd which seems to resent doing what it's told;

except in a bottom corner, where a singular blue figure
in a dunce's peaked cap and corset is
already ripping to pieces his banned book.

That one is Michael Scot of Peeblesshire:
who spurned his shepherd's birthright, and rode south
on a grey mare, after the star of knowledge:

to Oxford, where he bent the yew and the willow;
and Bamberg, a boom town, built on wizardry;
Toledo, where they forged his wand for him;

who pitched at last, astrologer at large,
into that crucible of the metric East
and Holy Rome that was Palermo then.

By day he would translate the secret books
of the Moor Averroes (who dared propose
sunlight between philosophy and God),

and went upstairs at night to play with fumes
and phosphor, and many a weird and future thing
hallooed from the pink mist of his magicking.

But when he once conjured himself, dead –
struck by a pebble, or mystery pellet – he quit
provoking heaven; took to the conical hat;

and broadcast those amends, by the despatch
in galley-chains of his appointed demon
to weave ropes of sand round the Bass Rock.

But the stone grew inwards. And the Florentine,
keeping a niche for everyone, has dropped
Michele without his brain in the Eighth circle,

among those seers, that for their forwardness
are trained to shuffle about with heads wrenched
back on their necks – rear-gunners, in hell-speak.

And worse: this shining, locomotive Scot
is strapped to the *Jimmie Mirror*, which lampoons
his magus as a slovenly patriot.

Guelf

Love moves the family, but hate
makes the better soldier;
why would the boxer scatter his purse,
sell up his soul, be Ugolino evermore,
for the soft-hard piece of his rival's ear –
were it not for the lovely taste of hate;
if it didn't award him a pleasant pillow
of hate to soften the stone of his cell?
Dante, who loved well because he hated,
Hated the wickedness that hinders loving.

Braveheart

(1329)

THE SPRING: – and as her ice draws off the glen
Scotland gets up, and is herself again;
Hawthorn has run in white to the riverside
Where bluebells crowd the bank, and the young Clyde
Skips down the hill with a fresh appetite
On stones as clear as the stars on a frosty night;
The hedge-birds hop and sing; the lambs uplift
Their heads, and try their legs; the odd miffed
Hare kicks shadows, while a spider trails her new
Laborious lifeline down the lanes of dew,
And all the deads of winter pass away
In Mary's month, the miracle of May.

But not in the royal infirmary at Cardross,
Where Robert Bruce lies mortally leprous:
Mumbling instruction – as around him droop
The flowers of his barony in a hapless group –
That when they send his carcass to the crypt
The heart should be removed, embalmed and shipped
On the pilgrimage his cares had kept him from,
And get its burial in Jerusalem:
Either before the Holy Sepulchre,
Where Mary Magdalen found her gardener,
Or in the thistled plot by the Dragon Gate;
And so in a borrowed year to wipe the slate

Of old offence – and speed his soul to God.
The voice failed; and the barons' general nod
Settled its grave injunction on Sir James,

Douglas 'the Black', a known keeper of flames
(Badge of the Douglases, a burning bonnet
With an unburnt salamander sitting on it).
And when no further pulse of him was heard
They took their dead king at his dying word
And from its shell of ribbed and yellow bone
The rough, distended organ was withdrawn
And packed in a hand-grenade of Ailsa granite
For transit halfway over the known planet.

~

THE NEXT SPRING: – and they gathered as decreed
Beside their boats at Berwick on the Tweed:
Sir William Keith, the Twa Lockharts of Lee,
And sixty more, sumptuous of pedigree,
Each with his *corps-des-armes* to man the deck;
And Douglas, with a heart around his neck.
Trimmed for the south, their sturdy fleet set sail,
Hauling its course through waterspout and whale,
Sea-wolves, and other monsters of the main,
Until they reached the sheltering coast of Spain
And climbed ashore, to fortify their will
Among the palms and fountains of Seville.

Ay, freedom is a noble thing . . . and these
Guid lairds have lent their men an evening's ease
To observe the local licence, and the sloth
That riots in the Sevillian undergrowth
Of tamarisk, wild figs and oleander;
So let us wink at Tam and Alexander
Crashing amongst the *vinos Andaluz*
To deaden the coming toll of Scottish youth;
Until the port bell chimes with the Angelus,

And someone snuffs a candle for the Bruce;
And soldiers fold, though morning vapours creep
About them, into nothingness and sleep.

Douglas said two words to his snoring men –
'Get up!' – and swept them to their oars again;
For while their morning-watch had blinked away
He'd had his breakfast with the teenage Rey
Of Gran Castile, Alfonso Love-the-Land,
Who'd shrewdly got 'the Black' to understand
That Osmyn the Orange, the five-hundred-acre
Lord of Granada, a Moorish troublemaker,
Had taken leave of his Arabian senses
And felled the uprights of their common fences
To extend his orange grove's perimeter
Beneath a crescent moon and scimitar.

Alfons, in a phrase that echoed through the heat,
Had vowed *to press these Moors beneath his feet*,
And urged his guests to play the white man's part
For all their urgent business of the heart.
Douglas lit up – a Christian leopard, he,
As ever he saw the cross in jeopardy –
Snatched at the chance to strike that heathen lord
With the sign of the Holy Rood and the broad sword,
And rowing his troops up a lethargic river,
The mazy, blockaged, rat-run Guadalquivir,
Disposed their arms, to toss his fortune's caber
In battle, near the burnt-out town of Teba.

Since here – in place of the proud Saracen
Of children's tales – a half-starved garrison
Peered from the gates, and on the summons made
Reluctant rows, like convicts on parade,

The Douglas, thinking the battle was in the bag,
Sounded his charge, and spurred his Solway nag
To bring it home; but on that foreign plain
The quivering mirage of the Moorish line
Ebbed and evaded his mounted men, who found
Their enemy had upped and quit his ground
Before they'd had a chance to kill him first;
And better judgment yielded to blood-thirst.

Alas for chivalry! This was the trick
Of feigned retreat, which, from the Arabic,
El Cid, at war a hundred years ago
With Moorish allies and a Moorish foe,
Had learned to keep a watch for; but the Scot,
Brought up on civil warfaring, had not.
Now both the observant chroniclers have said,
The Barbour and Le Bel, how Douglas read
Those buzzards round the sun as a fair sign
(The Douglas badge, described by Ballantyne
As 'a toad encyrcled by a flammand hat');
The Scots rode in pursuit, and that was that.

Wallop, and hiss, and fade. As waves break over
The Leith seawall, or froth the flags at Dover,
A tide of Moors swept round and through the force
Of dour, inflexible Scots and their spent horse.
Douglas, on his poor charger panicking,
Undid the pilgrim part of his late king,
Imploring, like a lamprey to the light,
'You, who were always first into the fight,
Our eager prefix, – *ay gannand afore* –
You get us out of this one, *Fortis Cor!*',
And wheeled his arm, and flung it, and before
It hit the ground the Douglas was no more,

But the shell burst. And what a heart it hatched!
Robert *Redux*, of nerve and muscle matched,
Who opened the pink gauze of his eyeflap
On vistas of olive toes and a sandalstrap
And shouted, – 'Get tae hell, ya Saracen git!
Mohammit gangs tae bed wi' a dummy tit!' –
Till seeing one Dervish pause in his footprints
To stamp his pound of offal into mince,
This remnant of our once and future Bruce
Set his survival skills to hyper-use:
Lay flat as fishies. Lay for a week, perhaps.
Then ached towards the north, trailing his pipes.

The Queen's Maries

There was Mary Seaton and Mary Beaton
   Mary Carmichael and me.
      – ANON.

Ye are na Mary Morison.
   – BURNS

'*Old, old, old.* It's all you ever hear
when you get to be eighty-three and deaf as a post –'
so no bad thing if she's doing all the talking
alone in her café at Dumfries bus depot;

and plenty to shout about, given her cancer,
'Titania' knees, failed blood, and a spleen saved
for the ministers of the Solway Health Authority:
'Pardon my French, but if for whatever reason

you happen to wander a foot off their prescription
by smoking a matter of forty or fifty a day,
they want sod all to do with you' – so saying
she disappears in a pall of her own making.

'I'm soft in the head, and know it, and wouldn't
completely disown it – seeing the rewards, if less,
are different – days when your friend's about –
your lambswool blanket – *Crossroads* – coffee – Bingo!'

   ∽

'What scares some people is losing their memories.
Fine, if you've got a particular story to tell,
but don't pretend they're gospel or gold coin,
mine anyway, mischief and rubbish, mostly.

My earliest one was always meant to be
this image of a train leaving a station,
the "Highland Brownie", namely, bound for Oban
out of Queen Street: the heads of the city boys,

wedged at the windows, shorn for the day, trailing
their bits of streamer, smaller and brighter now,
as the cars pull round and away beyond the brick.
Only one morning my sister says to me,

you couldn't have watched the Brownie – we
were *on* it – and describes the seats for proof;
so *fup*! – there it goes again, the faulty wiring,
the tinnitus, the memory playing tricks.

– Think of the moors at evening, when the mist
rolls over everything: you keep your head,
as long as you stick to the fog in front of you,
don't poke for a path round, through, or under it.

And what if we don't have larks – we nurse instead
internal nightingales, their *clank*, *tweet*
a boiler slowing down; as the Firth fades
at sunset, and clouds are the last things lit.'

∼

'This famous picture, then. Glasgow again;
and Scottish, of course, but also Victorian,
and painted, they said, before they raffled it,
not from the life, but rather historical.

On one side was the Black Mass of Dumbarton;
on the other, the masts of a gallery, too big for the harbour,
fitted for Brest and the French prince or Dauphin;
and in between a stretch of cobbles, laid

to shine in the rain and light, with the glimmer of scales
in a fish-market; and every stone, they said,
had another great painting painted inside it,
in microscope – the Last Fish Supper or whatnot.

It made me proud, me being a Mary,
like taking the star role in Nativity,
how the whole scene revolved around her halo,
that red-head: already no better, we saw,

than we should be, a mischievous spark of six: –
and the extras were just her train, the two or three
miniature lairds and the other infant Marys,
the guilty, bearded men bugging the background.

And surely it's nature, to sweep things together
when we look back; for then it was always
the future, limitless, chancy, and no contradiction
between being Mary and also one of the crowd.'

~

'Glasgow again, in nineteen forty-eight,
for Scotland–England: it's Solway grass, you know,
the sacred turf, the kissing turf; Hampden,
and Wembley too, came out of Cummertrees.

We were a hundred thousand, all of us Scots,
an army, like, but each his own commander;
we might have won, too, but for the goalie,
a lanky, unfortunate critter from Heart of Midlothian.

. . . By then it was over for us. He used to do
those French songs of the day, "Mimi", "Louise",
putting on his daft international accent;
it tickled me, all right: he was *my* Dauphin,

my own Chevalier. Him and his pals were part
of the Phibian Landings; not D-Day, but
a fortnight later – their pontoon was meant
to rebuild bridges behind the Canadians:

but the boat got shelled in the bay, he drowned,
they all drowned. And tell me if this is uncommon:
I loved him. I still love him, really. But then
I forget if he's Jackie or Hughie. – Here's the bus.'

~

Best and prettiest of Scottish names,
there are no new Marys anymore;
and this late flowering, after how many years
of making other people's beds in barracks,

hotels and hospices, got her modest send-off,
her jet brooch, bizzy lizzy and bus pass,
on the very day Mrs Thatcher decided
that any man over the age of twenty-six

who took the *bus*, could *count himself a failure*, –
whereas, she guessed, 'the clapped-out dames like us
were just coming into our own ("Excuse me, son,
these priory seats are reserved for me and my shopping!")'.

Thank heavens, likewise, for all the little girls
or not so little, ganging upstairs in a spiral
of swear words, text-tones, midriff and brutal candy
to back-seat country, putting as much distance

as buses allow between them and the elderly.
Some France they had: a dingy day out in a tunnel, –
but they tag on to the roll of great explorers:
'There was me, Shaneel, Shell and Michelle –'

Maroon

(1703)

It's just as well the man of Fife is neither
hostage to fancy, nor socially over-particular.
Before he is half-dry, he has put behind him
the rough justice you get as a sailor, and won't dwell
long on the rights and wrongs of his own case:

whether, in the Captain's terms, his Mate
was a bugger; or the Captain a thief, scanting
an honest Scot and his fellow mariner
of the spoil-share due to a crew member . . .
Indeed, it is only by seconds his second thought

when the *Mungo* pulls from the bay
that there's still plenty left of the day,
and since he unquestionably is marooned –
four hundred to the west of Valpareez –
he might as well settle to whittle the staves

of his new place: a basic shelter first,
until in time a house of logs should crown
all these unlikely acres. Looking up,
where a green cleft in the rock-face marks
his freshest water, berries that will be.

So, not for him the harrowing detailed once
on the next island, by a Dutch counterpart,
whose every prayer for a sheet or sail was fouled
by invisible spirits, hissing his offence at him
from behind boulders, or out of caverns. – No,

when the seals give up their morning holler
and slip into the warm Pacific, there remains
to the civilised ear, no sound but the shush
of wind in God's pimentos, or the light scree-shift
of high goats making themselves innocent.

                There on the damp walls
                    Of your ancestorals
            Rust hath corrupted the armour of Albin.
                Seize, then, ye madd'ning Macs,
                    Buckler and battle-ax,
            Lads of Lochaber, Breadalbane, Clan-Alpin!
                – OLD SONG

The Lost Leader

In which a fly
Pilots a dry
Course through rain
And back again.

And Micaiah said . . . I saw all Israel scattered upon the hills, as sheep that
have not a shepherd: and the Lord said, These have no master: let them
return every man to his house in peace.

        ∿

At Ruthven, by Spey ford,
It poured all day, around
The blown-up barracks, while we
Waited on your permission –
Sixteen hundred far-gone
Followers to the bone –
Until, at dusk, your plump
Liveried aide-de-camp
Wound up the slope
    On a yellow mare:

Who took as long as it took
To deposit, instead of an order,
Let each seek his own safety
The best way he can –
And down the hill again,
In coats of soaking silk.
We only had to weigh
That foreign sentiment,
That *sauve qui peut.*
    If we'd wanted to save ourselves . . .

Royal of him, as well,
That with that fleeting gesture
He sent a verse of Scripture,
A screed from Jeremiah:
Weep ye not for the dead,
Neither bemoan them:
but weep sore for him that goeth
away: for he shall return no more,
nor see his native country.
    – So how could he leave it?

That night I entertained
Shadows the weak lamp
Threw on the grey-green
Walls of the world:
A body that twisted,
Grew, and shrank.
Wind was the only sound,
With the rain in it
And once a dismal scrowl
    Of wild cats, mating or fighting.

The fire of belonging was out.
I saw my way, sticking
The course of the Tromie,
Up to a poor shift made
Between rain and wood,
And yours: west down channels
Of last-ditch loyalty;
To France at last, your safety,
Prince, Your Highness,
    Your brandy, gout and syphilis.

      ~

The cause was light,
A flower worn in the heart,
The secret white of the rose:
And all we did was sweetened by it.

Gray's Elegy

(1751)

Alas for this gray shadow, once a man
  – TENNYSON

Always that bit of him seemed somewhere else,
As if he'd come not from 'Two-bloody-A'
And *Cider with Rosie*, but from table-talk
With Lamb and Hazlitt; we guessed he was gay.

One time we wondered, 'What does it mean, the title,
Far from the *Madding* Crowd? Are the crowd mad,
Or are they making the other person mad,
So he's had to run away? Is he in hospital?'

'Fair question; but the man you'd have to ask
Is Thomas Gray' – and all the sharper boys
Pounced on the slip – 'You mean, Thomas *Hardy*',
And mocked him with a gentle *durring* noise.

'No, no, I don't. You see, while Hardy *chose*
His title, it was then the common course
When giving a book a name, to plagiarize
An apt quotation from another source.

As those who did "Fitzgerald and his World"
Will know, the title *Tender is the Night*
Derives from Keats; it wasn't Hemingway
For whom the bell tolled in the copyright;

And *Far from the Madding Crowd* is commandeered
From a very famous poem by *Thomas Gray* –
Gray's Elegy, is how it's known – which starts,
"The curfew tolls the knell of parting day . . .""'

He brightened briefly – 'Say we read it through –
To find what other lines this poem has lent!'
But there were no Grays left in the stock room,
So we talked about Hardy's wives till the bell went.

Not Jenny

To Chatham, where the great military mastodon
Musters to crush a distant colonial insect.
The King is hosting dinner. And through its hours and courses,
Its sculpted fats and fishes, eggs and roe,
Beauty-spots bob like shot in the eye.

Sunset. The port sways in candlelight; a steady
Slipping away, through narrow doors and passages,
Of men with order sheets, others with women or bottles.
The next day, the King might leave. Or stay.
For now, he gets in stages to his feet, to launch

On a speech which fails to deliver its trivial story –
How his mistress Jenny (now nudging his knee-bone)
Neglected to curb a pet gooze, a black gooze
That had fallen him   followed him   through the ways
Of a maze and it bitten him on the

– She has to join to steer him on, their voices
Clashing – 'His *Rear End*' – 'my be-behind!'
Till the joke wears audibly thin, and the King
Aborts to the toast, 'Not Jenny'. 'The *anti*-toast,
NOT JENNY', again, repeated till none take it up.

At which he has lost himself. Others, maybe,
Are wilder or worse, but there goes the King –
As if elsewhere, on the eve of scarlet adventure,
Up an unguarded inlet, a smeared nocturnal agent
Had snipped our row-boat from its reedy mooring.

The Ayrshire Orpheus

And down he went, sounding the deepest floors
Where Pluto ruled with serious Proserpine,
Still piping, till he reached their double doors
And knocked. And so he saw her, horribly thin:
Eurydice, her face all eaten in,
Curled at the feet of that disdainful pair
Who feigned surprise to see a Scotsman there.

Then Orpheus, soft and urgent, half in dread
Of what she had become: 'My bonny lass –
Hey – love – though it's better than being dead –
What's happened to your lovely lips and face?
How have they disappeared, or come to this?'
And she: 'Shoosh, pet, right now I dare not say –
But you shall hear the whole another day',

As Pluto intervened: 'Your silly wife
Has marred her face, and turned her belly barren,
Through dwelling on the home she may not have;
Mindful of Ballantrae and the view of Arran,
She finds the mills of Hell friendless and foreign;
If one could spring her now to the Ayrshire coast,
No doubt her looks would heal to their uttermost!'

So Orpheus sat before that mocking twosome
And let them have it, with his matchless voice,
Pitching 'Ye Banks and Braes' at the royal bosom;
A charming 'Ae Fond Kiss', and 'Ca' the Yowes',
And then 'My love is like a red, red rose';
Till Pluto swooned, and prickly Proserpine
Lay down her softening form upon the green.

The infernal lakes had filled with lily water,
Such was the gentle power of that recital,
When Pluto cleared his throat: 'I thank the Scot
Who wrote these songs, and you, who made them vital;
Name your own prize, and that shall be requital.'
And Orpheus begged, 'Then let me take my love
Back to that place we owned in the world above.'

Which tickled Pluto. – 'You're a bold one, Mac!
– Yet I'm inclined to grant such a request,
On this condition: should you once *look back*,
Your wife reverts to Hell of the heaviest!'
Then Orpheus clasped her freshening to his chest,
And up they strove, spiralling in their fate,
Till they had almost reached the outward gate.

If you have loved, imagine the sweet chat
The two then had, rejoining their own kind –
So can you blame him, in the midst of that,
If he should suffer a local lapse of mind?
I hate to say – she fell a yard behind –
Backward he blinked – chains belted from the deeps
And yanked Eurydice to Hell for keeps.

Poor Orpheus! He felt like some old town
Of Carrick in decline: Maybole, or Girvan,
The pubs shut down, the kids, taunting 'the clown
Who couldna face the front', on drugs from Irvine;
While dismal in the twilight of surviving
Alone with his shopping, sore to be rid of her,
He walks the roads of home a widower.

Diehard

(1832)

The young Scott, on a short lease at Lasswade,
Before he flit from poetry into prose,
Had tried his hand at breeding bantams – kinds

Of domestic fowl 'in which the cock is pugnacious'.
Only, through overbreeding, certain strains –
The Leinster Buff, with its tremendous neck

And breast, or the Scotch Grey – had grown effete,
And shunning a proud tradition, would rather flap
In circles round each other like big dusters.

Now Walter, whose own career in arms was curbed
In the right leg, by childhood polio,
Was game enough if a goose needed a boot;

And when the east coast flared with false alarm
Of a French landing, he formed with city friends
A legal militia, the Edinburgh Light Horse:

Saw action twice, helping to face down
Miners and mill-workers, but wore year round
Its scarlet uniform with sky-blue britches.

The Horse would laugh behind him, whether he led
Their exercise through Bonnyrigg, or growled,
Dismounting, at 'that infantry', their bairns;

While neighbouring farmers, though they loved no less
His songs and savoury stories, came to poke
Fun at the straighter face of the poultryman,

And when he lost a dozen birds to a fox,
Though all that time his run had been secure
'With wire intact to a height of three foot six' –

Gravely surmised, 'That maun be a *flying* fox';
'That, or maybe some gamefu' speerit has clapt
A pair o' wings on one o' your wee dugs!'

~

'*Testudo*' – as he signed one book review,
Alluding to the mode of the Tenth Legion
In Tacitus, of storming British positions

Beneath their shields, 'under a shield ceiling' –
Put up his nick-names, pen-names, *noms de guerre*,
'Shirra', 'My Landlord', 'Author of *Waverley*',

'The Wizard of the North', 'The Great Unknown',
And 'Laird of Abbotsford', as a plate of shields
From his mind's Melrose antique shop; as the means

Both to buy into and to dress the beams
Of that prose palace, his hobby and hungry folly.
And you might say, the Tweed's been up for grabs

Since tons of her softer, southern bank were forfeit
To Scott and a gas-lit Gothic anomaly. And yet:
When the capital comes, in golf-carts and garages

Rubbishing over the Abbotsford policies,
If the ghosts of Borders Past have kept a twelfth
Of the powers he assigned them in his *Minstrelsy*,

They'll yank the developers' feet from their four-by-fours
And shake them, till all the greed has chunkled
Out of the trouser bottoms – *yea, to the smallest change.*

For didn't he mind the crackpot and awkward acre,
Being, to hazard a swipe with a rusty phraser,
If not a *Nature's laird* then *bountiful maker*?

Look how he peopled the fields, they light up
When you say their names, *Dalgetty*, *Jarvie!*,
Not living, so much, as thoroughly acting the part,

With portable speeches and full stage-colouring:
Martyr and Highlander; lost children, heirs
To great estates; gypsies: Prince *and* Pretender.

The Scott novel's a 'Big Bow-Wow', shaggy,
Heavy, particular; slow to rouse; but once fixed,
Will not give up its grip on your reading leg.

    ∾

A son of the Manse, the painter David Wilkie
Would loiter in village fairs, or market places,
To execute in his Fife vernacular

The 'pauper style', learned from the Flemish (see
The Cottage Toilet, now in the Wallace Collection),
And so won youthful fame as the 'Scottish Teniers'.

In 1818, when our hero was offered,
And proudly accepted, the rank of Baronet,
Wilkie came over to paint a cabinet picture

Of Walter, his wife and weans as Border rustics:
Contrived by the painter this, by way of a break
From a weighty commission, *The Chelsea Pensioners*

Receiving the London Gazette Extraordinary
Of June the Twenty-Second, 1815,
Announcing the Battle of Waterloo,

For which the Duke of Wellington had advanced
Twelve hundred guineas – then a fantastic sum –
And that, they said at the *Heckler*, was just for the title.

(The kiss of death for Wilkie, a little later,
Was being appointed Royal Limner of Scotland:
For which there was no help but to depict

*The Entry of George the Fourth, in Highland Dress
To Holyrood House*, and render as rugged knee
The fat hock of Hanover; it wore the weeds

Of another formidable earner, but took him for ever,
Ate at his mind, fettered and followed him round
And turned out 'a horrible mixture of oil and water'.)

$\sim$

If Wilkie's star declined with the rise of Turner's,
The crash of Constable's washed Scott's, alas,
Unstable fortune in sheer lumps downriver.

$\sim$

For a few days, they say, he 'kept a face
Like thunder' – clicked his thumb ominously
At a black dog; but Scott would not go under.

One morning, he broke off the staring match
With bankruptcy – exclaimed to the family
'No! This right hand shall work it all off!'

Got up and (this was his finest hour) took seven
Even steps across the boards to his study, closing
The door behind him; just as if he meant

To collar the foam-jawed Beast of Debt in there
And tame her, with tickly, infinite strokes of his quill.
And truly, he wrote as long as he was able –

Not of his best – that went with the weathervane –
But colder things, to blunt the bills of ransom,
Napoleons, Demonologies, formula novels,

A difference lost on his detractors. 'Who now
Reads *Anne of Geierstein*?' Leavis would ask,
Deliberately choosing one of the least attractive,

As if his own tracts, while not exactly Gospel,
Or Acts, were forceful appendices tucked on these
– A tail. But who now reads *Revaluation*?

∽

We won't look away at the end. – You found
Reform, woo-wooing down the lanes
Of Hawick and Jedburgh, anathema,

And it snapped back at you. After the fourth
Aggressive palsy, your 'sagacious' face
Frozen beneath its shaven skull and skull-cap,

You speak less, and less well. You don't see
That both your boys fall in behind you, soon,
And childless, and the hard-bought title with them;

That the passage will turn out rougher, not moonlit
As you might have told it: trepanned, stupid
With opium, howl, howling for all that . . .

So while you can, Sir Walter, father-figure,
Stay with your stalwarts in a shaded room:
The silent deerhound, Maida; then a pair

Of that box-nosed terrier, known in the kennel
As aberdeens, but called by the Borderer
'Diehard', for their tenacity in the field,

Which might endear them to an ailing master.
That way, like Dandie Dinmont in *Guy Mannering*,
You come to lend your name to a whole breed.

Namely

Scottish Jews comin' doon frae the mountains
Minor prophets frae vennel and wynd,
 In weather as black as the Bible
  I return again to my kind
   – HUGH MACDIARMID

Few people thought Mick Imlah, who teaches at Oxford, was a
'Scottish poet'
  – ANGUS CALDER, *Scotland on Sunday*

'Angus Calder': it might have been piped by the Black Watch
or lowed by the Tweed; or plucked from the psalter of
 Hamish Imlach
(a singer so dyed in the cause, he was finally certified Scotch:
though less of a difference divides us than separates sameish
 and similar
– and besides, it was him, not me, they raised in the groves of
 Shimla,
while 'Sonny's Dream', his greatest hit, was Nova Scotian) –
but I've got this mongrel and seeming-Islamical M. IMLAH,
the SMITH, J. of phonebooks from Fez to the Indian Ocean.

For which I protest, there's a primary school near Edinburgh
that part of me never left, and cite my classmate Lorna
 MacDougall,
who grew up to share the name of the novelist Ishiguro,
'Ish' to his friends on the circuit, or point to the passage in
 Google
which proves IMLACH was what my family too had originally
 been,
Gaelic for *those of the loch*, until with the Clearance of Jura
the 'c' was lured from its croft by the trawlers of Aberdeen
and struck out o'er the moor, O.

So we've declined to this! – a prophet in black-face, fellow
to all those souls who have taken the bait of the Englisher
     Ashmole:
I wanted to play Macbeth, and they tricked me out as Othello
(*Makbeth*, in the Hebrew, is 'hammer'; *o' tellah*, in Farsi,
     'fishmeal').
And while my term is served, in a place off Portobello,
the woman who does my laundry unwittingly takes the
     Michael
by printing each week on the counterfoil for my wash-and-dry
     cycle
I, S, H . . . – I'll have to tell her. 'Don't call me Ishmael!!'

*And the King of Israel said unto Jehoshapat, There is yet one man,
Micaiah the son of Imlah, by whom we may inquire of the Lord: but I
hate him; for he doth not prophesy good concerning me, but evil. And
Jehoshapat said, Let not the king say so.*

Precious Little

By the shore of Lake Constance I sat down and prayed
That your health should not collapse in an African swamp.
I found the name you carved before I was born
On the Tower of Pisa, and chiselled mine beneath it.
When our hotel in Brussels burned to the ground,
I fled with nothing but my bullfinch and your portrait, dear.

Two dreams: that you have come home at last
With your throat slit, and walk past me without speaking;
Or, as I roam the poor quarters of Mecca or Medina
In my loose nightgown, exhausted with yearning,
I cry aloud, 'Does he care for me?' –
And think I hear an angel whisper, 'Yes'.

Begging

The job was, to eradicate deception
Amongst the beggars of the city: those
In earnest were entitled to their licence,
While cheats were to be cautioned, with a beating
Or a week in gaol, as they preferred, or both.

Me, I was clueless; till they teamed me up
With Dalton Bright, the 'Lambeth Labrador'.
Our first night out together, we found two
On crutches by the gates of Waterloo,
Boards round their neck like labels on decanters,

Declaring them A SAILOR OF THE FLEET
And SOLDEIR OF THE QUEEN. As we approached,
Dalton with real disgust said, '*He* a sailor?
Did you see him spit? He spat to windward.
A sailor would never spit to windward. Why,

He could not!' So the interview began:
What ship, what cargo, where . . . 'The Baltic, eh?!
Did you ever drink in the "British Flag" at Kiel?
What was the landlord's name? Was it not *Greaves*?
– You think so? – It was Baker. Leave your crutches.'

(And with a whipped seat stinging in his britches,
The sailor ran off with his legs.) 'And you, sir –
India – height of the Mutiny? Mmm, I guessed it
From the standard of your breath – which regiment
Was it you graced? Och aye! The Twenty-Third! –

The Lord's my Shepherd, Scotland forever, eh? –
You brazen impostor! The Twenty-Threes
Are the Royal Welch, and they did not go east
Till the June of Sixty-Five. I hate your sort!
Stand straight. Take off your hat. And beg directly.'

Rosebery

(Archibald Primrose, 1847–)

I'm not suggesting he was Oscar Wilde,
if I say, we all quoted him; he spoke
more squarely than that gentleman; besides,
his phrases had the stamp of mass production
and general currency – see, you probably
had one or two of them loose in your pocket:
nation of amateurs, ploughing his furrow alone.
And then his name, like Wallace or Wellington's,
crept into our streets and public houses:
he was the Earl of Rosebery, richest man
in Scotland; and, for an exacting year
and more, Prime Minister of the United
Kingdom of Great Britain and Ireland.

But there was one remark attributed
to Rosebery that I never liked (though why,
I wouldn't know till I was older), passed
at Parkhead, 1900: to the captain
of the Scottish eleven, which, taking the field
in Rosebery's racing colours of pink
and yellow hoops – he was their President,
but still, this seemed an honour overdone
to one not royal, exactly – had just thrashed
their English counterparts, four goals to one,
the greatest margin yet in the auld fixture –
holding his smile for the photographer –
'I haven't seen my colours so well sported
since Ladas won the Derby!' – *general laughter*.
(He'd left his Oxford college, not under

the usual cloud, but in a lord's dudgeon,
because the University rules required him
as an undergraduate, not to own a racehorse:
becoming an earl at twenty, he had said,
does not dispose 'one' to obedience.)
My thoughts were, then, that men should not be seen
in either of those two colours, or so nakedly
be made to run the race for someone else;
today, that he took one turf for another,
ours for his, and none had dared correct him.

Well, I had plenty to go on. My editor,
who'd used his club before the war, had warned me,
not disapprovingly, he could be cutting
and sarcastic: of his own wife, for instance,
as they left separately for a summer on Skye,
*Hannah and the rest of the heavy baggage
will follow later*; nor did he much enjoy
critical noises. But publicly he floated
on a cloud of pride, that bore him high and clear
like a balloon, whenever someone not
his equal – and surely few seemed otherwise –
appeared to him to be provoking him.

(At which he would lean back, hearing all this
quietly, only inflating slightly, as if to say,
'These' – quoting another – 'are certainly some
of my characteristics, and I glory in them.')

Known as unwounded, too – superbly so –
by innuendo, likewise implication,
he was forced (or so it seemed) to defend himself
in the skirmishes after the Queensberry hearing,
when rumours grew particular about himself

and the Marquess's son, and the blows got low
at the same time, round Rosebery's late wife.
Namely, as one of them dared in fact to put it,
'Why, sir, did you marry a Rothschild?' (meaning,
and understood to mean – *and one so plain
you can't pretend the attraction was natural*).
At which he glared for a moment at the questioner –
his eyebrows preternaturally still – and *quipped*,
would you believe, in the face of such ill-will,
'That we might lie together in life's index.'
Cool; pretentious; shutting them up for as long
as it took their wits to work it out; disdaining
to feed their envy. Then, '– Also, of course,
to get my greasy hands on the Mentmore stud.'

These were the means by which he kept warm
his authority, even when he was ailing.
At the hour of Armistice, which came, alas,
after his stroke – it rendered him speechless
into the autumn – and so failed to inspire him,
the whole host of Edinburgh gathered outside
his town house there, while he was propped upstairs
just semi-conscious – shouting out his name
like a football chant, *Rozbury, Rozbury,*
as if he'd scored twice on their piece of field.
And I suppose we will cheer for anything
that lets us own a bit of its victory,
even if it is stricken or so struck
it can't get to the window to wave back
or utter a word to clinch the occasion.

So whether, indeed, his powers of recovery
'confounded his physicians', or with the loss
of finer faculties, as one reported,

he'd 'hardened into dogma', either seemed
to me a daunting prospect: he took on
the character of the headstrong general,
let down, scathing of both sides – but showing
his utmost in the fog and shame of retreat.

And that was when I met him – or, rather,
he allowed me half an hour out of a day.
It was a new thing then, the interview,
brought from America, like women smoking,
but hardly subversive, yet: the courtesies
would still apply, not least in this case.
All morning I'd felt as you do in dreams
when it's time for you to take the penalty,
but the ref has lost the place, the big keeper
keeps stalling, there's a minor crowd invasion,
and even as you begin your run-up a crow
has settled impertinently on the ball;
till at last I was set, after a train down
from Waterloo to Epsom, on the private
crescent of budding limes that led around
to the front of Durdans – his 'out-of-London' house.
It was late April, and a lovely day:
low sun, light wind, daffodils everywhere,
and barely a hint of egg-and-bacon hoops
in the tufts of lambswool cloud that fringed the sky.
Classically fine: but silent, too; as if
the birds had been flushed off the property;
1919, the winter's virus still
camped on the downs, it felt that everything
English was exhausted. Except for this,
which tells you just how far we stood away
from Russia yet: that here, one kind of man

with both his legs, if now lame in the left,
and multiple homes could still expect to bathe
in a freshening pool of national sympathy.
As if we knew, and let it matter, that
he'd been unhappy, in all his place and riches.

Stick to the questions. So I ran them through,
scraping my cane along the sweep of gravel:
Do you regret your ministry was not
a longer one – though so much was achieved?
– or, Was it the splits within your own party,
or the Irish crisis, more, that brought you down –
no – *that we should blame the more for your*
untimely exit? ('Neither. The truth is,
I had to get out sharp, I was seeing things') –
And in retirement, what . . .

                                   When in breezed
his amazing daughter. 'How d'ye do!
I'm Peggy Crewe – You must be – Modicum . . .'
– offered her hand, and gave me such a smile
I must have said, indeed I was – I watched
the daisies on her dress – She held her smile;
and as her hand withdrew, I was wondering
at the way this being shone in her station,
whose grace was almost natural, almost
the real thing; and, how I would be the first
to fall in behind her lead or standard –

'But go straight through, he'll be expecting you –
and don't let him start on the spring flowers!'
I barely heard; and then with perfect timing
she'd disappeared. – Yet when I knocked
and entered he was already talking in that
maimed magnificent voice, emphatically, as if

to a nurse or a second invalid concealed
round the dog-leg of the sports or morning room;
to someone who had gone too far
with *primula*, as a name – 'a silly name';
and '*If* I call them primroses, it is
because that is *exactly* what they are.'

London Scottish

(1914)

April, the last full fixture of the spring:
'Feet, Scottish, feet!' – they rucked the fear of God
Into Blackheath. Their club was everything:
And of the four sides playing that afternoon,
The stars, but also those from the back pitches,
All sixty volunteered for the touring squad,
And swapped their Richmond turf for Belgian ditches.
October: mad for a fight, they broke too soon
On the Ypres Salient, rushing the ridge between
'Witshit' and Messines.   Three-quarters died.

Of that ill-balanced and fatigued fifteen
The ass selectors favoured to survive,
Just one, Brodie the prop, resumed his post.
The others sometimes drank to 'The Forty-Five':
Neither a humorous nor an idle toast.

The Bright Side

Ach, don't keep on
At the seaside Scot
For his daytime drinking;
Better than not.

Look on the bright side.
Think of the future;
Picture a ghost
With a hand like paper

Pegging you back with
'Hi, I'm Mac –
A reformed alcoholic!'
(Ghastly, earnest) –

Picture his eyes
(Pin-clear, pleading),
Think of a night
Like a Bible Reading –

And view the unseasonal
Clown on the pier
('I only get drunk, ooh,
Twice in the year –

Hic! – Tober to May,
And May to October!')
In kindlier light
(At least he's not sober).

Drink v. Drugs

I was worked up about some other matter
when I saw that phone box off the Talbot Road
being smashed outwards by someone inside it,
after closing on Sunday (Sunday's the day
they all go mad on crack); which is why
I didn't as usual walk by on the other side
but advanced with a purpose, and as he swivelled
nonchalant out of the frost, grabbed his lapels,
and setting him roughly against the railings,
'What is it with you,' I asked him, 'drugs?' –

which I knew very well from his vacant expression;
and after he'd cautioned me weakly
against tearing his coat, the stoned boy
answered, matter-of-factly, 'Yes' –
and told me which ones, in a Liverpool accent.
It was here I think I said something stupid
about rugby v. football, which he ignored,
rallying rather to call me a prick
and a Good Citizen, and I thought, never mind,
I'm still going to call the police.

But that would have meant myself going into
the vandalised box, and releasing my hold,
which maybe he saw, with his pert 'Go on then';
then, something better came into his head,
that *he* would phone, since he hadn't done nothing;
and moments later he was giving the station
the lowdown on the guy in a light blue shirt
and black jeans who'd assaulted him, seeming
the worse for drink, and accused me of smashing

the phone box from which he was calling now.
When in fact I'd begun to warm to the lad –
who'd flattered my stab at authority, kept
a lid on the thing; also I couldn't be sure,
could I, that he hadn't been simply clearing away
glass that was broken already, with strong
but not violent blows of the phone.
In any case, when he started to amble off,
I did nothing to stop him; and when the blue
light came quietly round the corner I was standing
alone with nothing to say for myself but my name.

Past Caring

As a ship
Sees only the tip
Of the ice's pyramid
That has already scraped her bows,
We'd glimpsed that drink was something you overdid;
Now after the wreck I sift the damage you'd stowed in the house.

Eyes glazed
I fumble, amazed,
Through mounds of knickers and slips,
Extracting the bottles you'd buried there; these
I hump in their binbags, clashing against my knees
To the 'bottle bank', by the public baths; it takes four trips.

The gin!
No wonder you're thin;
Hundreds of bottles of gin;
And feeding them singly into the ring
My arm grows weary from shifting the bottles of gin;
A numbing collection of lots of exactly the same thing.

You were vain
As you went down the drain;
Why else would you lay up this hoard
If it wasn't one day to take stock as I'm doing
Of what an almighty amount you had taken on board?
And here am I turning your trophies to scrap at an illicit viewing!

A smear
Of lipstick, here –
Like the kiss on a valentine;
And sniffing the neck I feel suddenly near to you,
For what it gives off is your smell, if we kissed any time,
And it wasn't a cheap perfume – but the only thing properly dear
    to you.

Next week
If you're not past caring
They may let you out for an airing,
To slump in your armchair, too burgled to speak,
The fish out of water that stubbornly stays all the more fish:
Then how shall we drag the treasure you were back to the surface?

Stephen Boyd

(1957–95)

And on thai went, talkand of play and sport . . .
    – HENRYSON, *Orpheus and Eurydice*

I can't drive, and I dreamt that I was driving
Unstoppably through a succession of red lights
Till I hit that slow-moving Transit amidships –
A crash that must elsewhere have killed somebody.
So I was doubly relieved, when the smoke cleared,
To see it was you who climbed unhurt from the van,
Fuming: you, who I knew to be dead already;
For though the SALTIRE overlaid your face,
The funeral mask of Scotland's Everyman,
Those specs and spry moustache gave you away –
Those, and the warmth in your abuse of me –
And it seemed from how your empty trousers scissored
And slipped through the ground, the dream after all
Was benign; they'd made you a sort of wizard.

I first ran into you in '82,
In Oxford, when you came over the road
From a rival college, to do graduate work
In Magdalen MCR: four pints a night,
Electric-thin, brimful of mimicry,
With a laugh that stopped unnervingly – .
We might have kept suspiciously apart:
You a Glaswegian from the Irish side;
Me, from the softer suburbs of the Kirk,
Who hadn't knowingly met a Catholic boy
Till I was sent to have my tonsils out
In the Ear, Nose and Throat on the Paisley Road

Aged seven, where the alien ward was full
Of green favours, Celtic scarfs and scruffs;
And years of a Southern education since
Had trimmed my Scottishness to a tartan phrase
Brought out on match days and Remembrance Days.

So football, I'd assumed, would be your game –
Not the perversion I was public-schooled in;
Until, one evening's ending at the bar,
Jocking it up, I 'prophesied' aloud
The 'greatness' of some teenage Border prospect,
Saviour of Scottish rugby and so on –
And you stepped out of the wan group you'd adopted,
With that particular look you had, half doubt,
Half reckless allegiance; the look, in fact,
Of the early Christian in the film *The Robe*,
Patrolling Nero's streets, when his ear catches
In a slave's whistle from the sewer beneath
A Hebrew melody gone underground:
The trace-note of some fellow in the faith.

Those days, the Scots lost more games than they won,
But the playing parts were mightier than the sum:
The last sparks of the cherub Andy Irvine,
My mother's favourite, 'out of Heriot's';
The hooker, Deans, pent-up, belligerent;
The steep kicks of our fly-half, Rutherford
('That one's come down with snow on it, I'll tell you');
Paxton the number eight, who on the box
Was always 'thumping on' or 'smashing on';
And Leslie, the deadly flanker from Dundee.
You also liked that Catholic lump from Hawick,
Shonnie McGaughey, who in the national side
Revelled in having bridged the great divide.

This is a long poem for a friendship based
On little more than aping Bill McLaren,
And spelling out again that sport matters
Because it doesn't matter; by such a ruse,
If not for long, worse things could be postponed. –
Meanwhile, two prigs, we liked to disapprove
Of those who showed their fears or bared their heart;
As when, in one of your fancier flights,
You said of the social posture of a scholar
Whose girlfriend had gone off with someone other,
That he 'expects the whole community
To circulate his sorrow, open-mouthed,
Like the wee Marys in Giotto's *Crucifixion*!'

The problem was, that day in late November,
When flu had scrubbed out half of Magdalen's strength,
To get fifteen of any ability out
To take on Balliol; when you piped up
Unhelpfully, 'I'll play' – yet there was no one else.
So we put you at full-back, farthest away
From the kick-off, at least; you had arrived
In a pair of khaki shorts (we played in black),
Which in a private reference to the kilt
You wore with nothing underneath, and kept
Your heavy-duty glasses on as well;
I'm sorry, but you looked ridiculous.
Ten minutes in, nil-nil, my hamstring went,
And we were down to fourteen – or, thirteen
Plus you. And yet, although you couldn't 'catch
To save your life', today you rescued Magdalen.
You pouched their box-kick with a booming 'Mark!',
Tackled and got to your feet and tackled again,
Swearing in Scots, and in attack made one

Comedian's charge through their amazed three-quarters.
I thought you'd crack in the second half; you didn't;
Not when a bonfire spread the field with smoke,
Or the light faded, towards the final whistle.
Six-three to us: a try by David Gearing.
Now I pull muscles sprinting in my sleep
And you make probing runs from the deeper deep.

Two white diagonals on a field of blue:
The Saltire, or the *crux decussata*,
Banner of *Braveheart* and the Glasgow Kiss,
Is said to represent the wooden X
To which, one morning by the harbourfront
At Patras, they attached our patron saint,
The first disciple, Andrew of Galilee,
Fisher of Men, called 'Manly' in the Greek:
Then seventy, a good age for a martyr.
We see it in the struts of a hurdle gate;
We saw it in the angles on the blackboard
Of the attacking full-back and his wing
When scissoring or dummy-scissoring.

A warm deceptive spring followed the March
Of David Sole's Grand Slam in 1990;
I flew up to St Andrews, where you'd won
A fellowship in English, and got married
To Sue the musician; since somehow you'd fixed it
For the powers-that-be up there to pay me
To do a poetry reading with Kathleen Jamie.
Our lives had changed, or yours had changed especially,
But still we had our taste for the old routine;
In the Indian afterwards, you leant forward
To murmur, like an arch-conspirator,
'I predict greatness for Damian Cronin' –

A good hard lock, though frequently overweight,
In and out of the side till his knee gave way
In '98 – and never quite as good as great.

Of all your flawed predictions, this was the last,
That I remember. Soon we'd got the bus
Back to the pretty house you'd bought in Crail,
A fishing village with a postcard harbour,
And hit the whisky, you harmlessly hammered
In front of your wife; till the turning point
The pleasure ended, or pretending did.
You'd put a record on, of Monteverdi,
Or something even earlier, singing yourself
In a passionate, reedy voice – and weeping, lots,
Then weeping more; and Sue had arms around you,
Stroking and shooshing, but without surprise –
So this was not the first time, nor the last.
She made you steady, and I went to bed,
And slept; but it resumed – whispers, breaking –
You exclaiming – she hushing you down –
And when she brought my morning tea, you'd gone.

I heard you had two boys ('just thirteen more . . .'),
But didn't write; and then your colleague phoned
To say he understood that we'd been close
(I heard you bristle back, 'We were *not close*'),
And that he was afraid you'd 'Taken Your Life' –
Preferring not to say in which specific
Knock-kneed, hurtful, individual style.
It doesn't matter. And I wouldn't force the door
For one cartoon, Body with rocks, bottles,
Or railway track, to blot out what you were;
But while we're at it, I'd be pleased to know
Your standpoint on the new Cronin, Scott Murray,

Whose jumping in the line-out begs comparison
With the Spey salmon; and to square with you
The lessons I was meant to take away
From our phantom collision: not to let die
The memory of your glorious afternoon
V. Balliol; and not to dwell on loss
If your sons' path and mine should ever cross.

Gordon Brown

(Rugby player – 'The Ayrshire Bull' – d. 2001)

Their gratitude for your career was such
That when some District prop in his narrow pride
Stamped on your head, and legged it into touch,
The Board banned *you* (that's rugby suicide):
Who blew through London Scottish on the breeze,
When I'd been training with the fourths or thirds
And dreamt you said *I'd like to meet him, please!*,
Till someone drew me in, and we had words.

You knew two bits of Burns. Still you pretended
Poems would outlast what the British Lions did,
You, who had beaten Springbok and All Black;
And when you put your spare hand on my back
I felt at first a woman, then a kid,
And then a man, the thing you had intended.

Maren

You saw so much romance in competition,
like Atalanta before you – daughter
of thick-witted Schoeneus, a Boeotian –
they said you'd marry anyone who beat you
in a footrace. Hence our peculiar courtship:

you, crowned once the fastest girl over
three thousand metres in Lower Franconia,
myself the great Caledonian bore,
we took to jogging round the astroturf
of Wapping's amenable sports arena.

Plainly, you could have romped ahead
at any point; instead, you made me lead,
woman after my own heart! – dropping
your courteous metres back, as if
feeling the pace, an arrangement

you gilded with 'I can't keep up
when you accelerate!' So we complete
our sixth or seventh lap of the course;
and only when I flag, an end in view,
near to the bags and coats, do you appear

flush at my ear, demanding 'more!'
Together, then, after our fashion:
exchanging oaths like old antagonists,
your Focke-Wulf tailing my Spit
into fresh air and another orbit.

Iona

Where are you taking us, sir?
the crew needed to know;
but since by the final day
    my guiding star,
instinct and purpose both, had strayed so far
off the monitor – I found I couldn't stay
    for fear of the answer.

    To tell the truth
I had given up on youth; would only stew
in the chemical toilet, the door half-
open, a 'cry for help', till out of the blue
    a nurse ducked
from the cockpit holding you, and I
was face to face with my pilot!

    ∾

In the weeks before you were born
    the head did warn
me not to give over the stage at once
to baby talk: and so we stood our ground
when from among your breathings-out were told
    two voluntary sounds,
a rudimentary yes and no.

But now, when all the words
we care about are yours, I have to tender
    our deep surrender;
as in a suit of dungarees you go
    groping your way to sense
like Milton, blind before he felt
    the wall's resistance.

～

Already you discern what the artist meant
in an old poster of mine, the 'Mars'
of Velazquez: the war god in his afterprime
    released too soon
from that perpetual service; sat
in his demob nakedness and gloom,
only his helmet on, almost
a souvenir, muscles smoking away,
    until you up and say
– *Poor tin soldier man!*
He's thinking about things!

～

My right hand is Nessie's head,
her neck my dripping arm. *How old*
is the dinosaur? Forty
    or fifty million years.
Can the dinosaur sing? No,
too old; but likes to be soothed
    by others singing.

I open her thumb-
    and-finger beak
at least to let her speak
in her quavery Triassic,
'Take me to your leader!'
– to which you instantly,
    I haven't got any leader.

～

What, meanwhile, are my own terms?
Darling – 'little' – *Mädchen* – the same
Suspicious argot I used to spy on.

∽

Strange, that we dwell so much
sometimes, on self and such,
that we can spend an age without
    a clear view out:
when, if I asked the mirror once
in the way of an old queen,
to frame how things might look
twenty or thirty visits thence,
all it reflected back was white
and unrefracted light, the mean
prophetics of a closed book.

Of course, it was not allowed to show
    or we to know
that you were coming all the time,
    my perfect rhyme;
how you would seize the reins, Iona,
riding my shoulders over the hill
    or rarely sitting still,
your hands spread on my knees, my jeans
    the sidelines of your throne.
Succession is easy: first it was them,
then me for a bit; and now it's you.

∽

Granted your repertoire
        has lumps in it,
of Shrek and Cinderella;
but there's prodigious poetry too,
        a magic spring
in the sweet Cordelia thing
you once undid me with –

Let's laugh through all the days, till the water
        comes over our eyes . . .
or, which is more my line – not
mawkish, I think, or maudlin:
In Oxford Church, there are two Marys;
        one of them has got a baby
and one of them hasn't got a baby.

I In Memoriam Alfred Lord Tennyson

(d. 6 October 1892)

> I remember once in London the realization coming over me, of the
> whole of its inhabitants lying horizontal a hundred years hence.
> – TENNYSON, quoted in Audrey Tennyson's notebook

No one remembers you at all.
　　Even that shower of Cockney shrimps
　　Whose fathers hoisted them to glimpse
Your corpse's progress down Whitehall

Have soiled the till and lain beneath
　　While the last maid you kissed with feeling
　　Is staring at the eternal ceiling
And has no tongue between her teeth.

Now sanctified are your remains:
　　The poems; Hallam's obedient book;
　　The photographs your neighbour took
Of an old Jesus with food stains;

The rest is dressed up decently
　　And drowned, as surely as your son's
　　Untimely coffin, that flashed once
And slipped into the Indian Sea.

You are not here; you cannot fall.
　　So let the mighty organ blare!
　　While we, who plainly were not there
Construct this fake memorial.

～

In the hope of finding something that might flesh out my phan-
tom Tennyson Centenary project, my girlfriend drove me one
evening down to Aldworth in Sussex, the poet's second home
and the closest of his haunts to London. We had read of the
new owner's excessive hostility to visitors, but she wasn't
deterred, on my behalf, by the height of the gate or by the
notice of watchdogs. So I followed her suggestion to break
into the garden, and carried the torch down a path which gave
me a dim view of the front of the house, from about fifty
metres, across a minefield of lilies and a steaming pond, and
absorbed this for a minute before heading back to join her on
the drive. But even as my feet landed again on common gravel,
she screamed – not at the flash of what seemed like theatrical
lightning but at something on my blind side it must have lit up.
So I turned to confront what I guessed in that instant was
either our man with a shotgun or an earlier intruder strung up
by his heels.

∿

Cannot you, as a friend of Mr Tennyson, prevent his making such a
hideous exhibition of himself as he has been doing for the last three
months? . . . I thought there was a law against indecent exposure.
  – SWINBURNE to Lord Houghton

When fifteen men were charged at Bow Street Court on Monday
after a disturbance around Eros, in Piccadilly Circus, it was
mentioned in court that one of them claimed to be Lord Tennyson.
Lord Tennyson wishes to state that the man was not in fact Lord
Tennyson, and has no connections with him, and that he does not
know him.
  – *The Times*, 1 January 1948

∿

I knew him at once – for a student, or out-of-work actor, or
    worse,
With Tennyson's frock and fedora, and a volume of Tennyson's
    verse,
But even the mouldiest music-hall turn would be sunk from the
    start
By a stature at least seven inches too short for the laureate's
    part.
This was a bloke whose Kraken had woken for years twice a
    night
In some shallow provincial canal; and when he began to recite,
The personal touch of the door-to-door salesman could never
    obscure
That this was the fiftieth one-to-one Tennyson show of the tour.
'Mr Imlah! The warmest of greetings, good sir, from myself and
    the Queen!
I'm Alfred, Lord Tennyson – dare I suggest that you know who
    I mean?
So relax – and unlock the front gates of your mind – for tonight
    I arrive
To proclaim as I did once before – The Dead Are Not Dead But
    Alive!'

∽

. . . the full, the monstrous demonstration that Tennyson was not
Tennysonian
    – HENRY JAMES, *The Middle Years*

(Oscar Browning introduces himself):
O. BROWNING: I am Browning.
TENNYSON: No you're not.
    – E. F. BENSON, *As We Were*

This is the most extraordinary drawing. It is exactly like myself.
    – TENNYSON on a portrait of the dead Dickens

∽

'The trick of the afterlife is – that what you sign up for, you get,
Which as in the case of Tithonus, we have leisure enough to
    regret.
Ours is a sepia parlour, a club without pipes or the port,
Half full of identical males, where Her Majesty still holds court.
As we strut in our standardised jacket, beards on our
    standardised face,
Dickens and Grace and myself are dubbed the Three Graces –
    by Grace.
There isn't a future in Heaven; no nightclub, or pool with
    jacuzzi –
You walk in the garden with Gladstone, or stand at the piano
    with Pusey.
And yet, while we keep the old pastimes, we keep the old
    dread:
And that, for our sins, is an absolute terror of being dead.
These days we can hardly get four for bridge; I've seen the
    departure
Of Lytton – accepted – but *Manning*, by God, and Macaulay,
    and *Archer*!
They're all cast over the margin and into the beggarly throng
Who bray for biography, down in the darkness, all the night
    long.
My Arthur – poor angel, I did what I could – I see in fits:
His wings gone limp with disuse, and the plumage in ribbons
    where bits
Of his carcass stick out like spokes of a battered and bandaged
    umbrella.
His features appear where he gnaws at the grille of his terrible
    cellar,
Fading and growing and fading again with never a sound,
And but for my friendship his luminous half-life would choke
    underground.

'Tonight there was dancing in heaven – jigs with Elizabeth
    Siddal.
But after an hour on the fringe of events, and her in the middle,
I suddenly hated the uniform steps and the scrape of the fiddle,
And staggered out dizzily into the thick of the alien stars,
Shouting my name, till Hesperus fetched me in one of her cars
And dropped me on Earth for the evening. I'm saved. And to
    hell with the distance –
There's times when you've got to get out amongst folk to
    promote your existence.'

And now from the folds of his frock coat he conjured the book,
    and affected
A cartoon myopia, cribbed from its cover (the Penguin
    Selected),
'And so to that end it's my pleasure to read to you – starting
    with: *Maud*.
I hate –' But I couldn't take more of this – be it dementia, or
    fraud,
So I hushed him abruptly and fished out a quid for the
    in-patients' kitty
And gathered my girlfriend to make our way back to her car
    and the city,
Casting a jibe at him over my shoulder – 'You're not Lord Ten-
    nyson!' –
Catching the small, disembodied retort, 'Well, neither's Lord
    Tennyson.'

∽

Tennyson at a seance –
A great poet, lest we forget,
And certainly one of the most haunted –
Before all the others had settled,
Cried out in a cracked voice,
'Are you my boy Lionel?'
And got
Not
The reply that he wanted.

ii 'B.V.'

> If circumstances had been smoother and brighter about him . . . he would have had what was much needed in his case, a more spacious home.
>
> – GEORGE MEREDITH, letter to Henry Salt, 1 September 1888

The Walker

> Had I but means and a free mind
>   You'd never tie me to one bed
> For I should wander unconfined
>   And virgin paths should feel my tread
>   – JAMES THOMSON, unpublished fragment, Dobell MS

Things being worse, while I must creep
   Each evening back to Pimlico
Still I can leap before I sleep
   Through Hampstead Heath, or Barnes, or Bow,

Unless THE CLOUD resume its place
   And the rains rain gutterly;
For then I pace my given space –
   Three by four, four by three –

And feel akin to the caged creatures
   In Regent's Park: to the roofed-in
Eagle with the impacted features,
   Or the brown bear in his bear-bin

Who rocks upon a yard of slate
   With room for three of his four paws,
Shifting his weight to simulate
   The bearing of the thing he was.

An Invitation

Kirby Muxloe, Leics.

Friend, come and stay awhile; Miss Barrs and I
    Crave the refreshment of your company;
And if, of late, your old unhappiness
    Has made you sick, better to convalesce
Where we can nourish you with country things,
    Like Leicester beans and bacon – 'food of kings',
And the best smell the subject ever smelt;
    Pork pies from Melton Mowbray, pies that melt,
Crust, meat, and jelly, in the crowded mouth;
    Pickles from Branston Valley to the south;
Stilton, or *Quenby,* judged 'the greatest cheese
    In all the world' by local authorities;
And the fat capon from the farmyard, done
    In wine and lemon – or lemon and tarragon.
Thence to the [non-!] smoking room, where we may pass
    Hours with the couplet rather than the glass,
And put old Horace right ('No poem lasts long
    That hath been writ on *aqua*' – doubly wrong,
Steeped as he was in the Pierian Spring);
    And last, with nightcaps on our heads, we'll sing
Accompanied purely by my father's daughter,
    To prove the lyric qualities of water.

Homely amusements! – and they may read mild
    To one whose nature has run wholly wild;
But look: we have a thousand acres here
    Of fern and gorse, and ancient oak, and deer,
To ramble where you will; and in such grounds
    Your spirit may shake off the ghostly hounds

That haunt you into illness. Come, be calm;
    Do odd jobs, if you like, around the farm,
Feeding the chickens, or collecting wood;
    And if your pledge of abstinence holds good,
The Fates may yet extend their benisons
    And *Thomson*'s star be twinned with *Tennyson*'s
A hundred years from now. So come, my friend,
    As soon as possible; come next weekend,
When Harry's children will be up with him –
    Who love you, James, as much as you love them.

– J. W. BARRS to James Thomson, 28 March 1882

∿

Sir,

You will appreciate that your presence is no longer to be tolerated in this house. Since your own apparatus will doubtless be unable to reconstruct the events of the early hours of this morning, I should record: i) that earlier in your stay Miss Barrs had discovered flasks of what we take to be brandy concealed in the outbuildings – ii) that you went out with your pipe after supper and – despite our search and shouted entreaties – did not return at least until after we retired which was as late as midnight – and iii) your worse than nauseous condition – *before the children* – when you at last unlocked your door this morning – which, taken together, prove your vow broken and our trust betrayed, – with what dreadful consequences.

As you pertly said before you disappeared, you cannot, with your means, hope to make recompense for the loss of 200 fowl, or for the damage the fire has done to the brooder house. Neither is it meaningful to 'thank' us for past kindnesses, as if these should be endlessly repeated. I cannot wish you ill, only that you were better. But I despair of you.

– J. W. BARRS, draft of letter, spring 1882; not sent

Nowhere is the verse feeble . . . the majesty of the line always has its full colouring, and marches under a banner. And you accomplish this effect with the utmost sobriety, with absolute self-mastery.

    – GEORGE MEREDITH, letter to James Thomson, 27 April 1880

No news – except that he is still on the warpath and in very full paint.

    – H. HOOD BARRS, letter to J. W. Barrs, 17 April 1882

Dear Mr Barrs,
                Alas! – I'm afraid I was squiffy myself,
When I offered to ride to his rescue. – Still, I was hot on the scent;
For I followed that dog-eared stub of address to a Pimlico
    roomhouse,
In the shade of a railbridge spattered by pigeons, and rapped at
    the door
At nine in the morning on Monday – the likeliest hour of the
    week.

The landlord is GIBSON, an irascible type with an air of long
    suffering,
Who as I pronounced the offending initials stepped back with
    a snort –
And then, with sarcastic good manners, conducted me through
    to the scullery,
Where *guess what* had happened – the walls scorched, the floor
    awash
With charred rags, and chairlegs, and offal and cabbage, all
    sodden and sooty.

It appears that at five this Gibson had woken with smoke in his
    nostrils
And stumbled downstairs, grabbing at buckets of slop as he went,
To discover a fairsized bonfire ablaze in the heart of his kitchen,

And our hero, impassively viewing the scene from the warmth
    of an armchair,
Offering never a word of excuse – only after a while,

And then, very often, shouting out 'Heebson! *Olé! Olé!*
Señor *Heebson! Olé!* – alluding, I learned, to a wild
But unshakeable fancy of his that the landlord was secretly
    Spanish.
(*For reference* – it seems the said Spaniard had dared in the
    earlier evening
Engage with his crapulous lodger on matters of *rent* – hence this.)

So Gibson had chucked him out 'sharp', and was voluble now
    in relief,
Being rid of that 'stink', as he put it, for good – crowing,
    indeed,
That if ever that 'B—' should darken his doorstep again, by
    G—d,
He could count on a merry reception, etc. I bid him good day
And was happy for that to remain the extent of our novel
    acquaintance . . .

But I hadn't been home for an hour, when Gibson came
    knocking at *mine* –
For listen – the whole of the time he'd been cursing the fellow
    to hell
B.V. had been upstairs asleep, in one of the unlet rooms!
Since G. in the heat of his temper had failed to recover *the key* –
Our Homer had simply slipped in while he fumed at his coffee
    and kippers!

This time, he went meekly, it seems – though leaving his mark
    on the bed –
Remembering, he claimed, that he'd business to see to, with
    'friends in the park'

Which G. took to mean with 'his brethren, them beasts what
   they keep behind bars'.
Since then, I report, no one's seen hide nor hair of him –
   living or dead –
Including
         Yours Truly
               I wish I was sorry to say.

   – PERCY HOLYOAKE to J. W. Barrs, 17 April 1882

~

'He's been taken very ill,' I urged. 'He can do no harm now. Won't
you take him in if we bring him?' The man emphasized his refusal
with an oath, and slammed the door.
   – T. E. CLARKE, account of events of 1 June 1882

With money, I believe I should never have a home, but be always
going to and fro the earth, and walking up and down in it.
   – JAMES THOMSON in conversation

~

The Library

GENTLEMEN ARE REMINDED
THE READING ROOM IS NOT A HOSTEL
on barred doors, at midnight;
beside it, LIVE THIS EVENING:
THE AUTHOR OF 'INSOMNIA',
'THE WALKER', 'IN MY ROOM', ETC. –

the very man who now hogged the portal, –
head first, as if to butt in five hours late
on his own abandoned reading,
but not so much as breathing
through the mask of custard, brandy, blood
his spatchcock nose had blurted.

[126]

Yet stooping as I did
to find what work-in-progress
had stopped in those pockets,
the eyes in the back of my head
detected a thing less dead, –
a statue, hard by –

a stray from the museum:
but on its brow, there blew a live
crown of leaves; and the wind's pulse
rippled its grooves of gown;
and when its finger moved to fix
the wet clay I straightened from,

a stone voice ground out at me
(in English, with a marble accent),
'Relieve yourself, now, on this head's flesh,
The quicker to melt it into mulch and aether –'
(so anxious to obey, I looked to see
I was already doing as he instructed)

'– For a reputation spoils in the stacks
With fox marks on the pages, and this
Oaf's glandular grin for a frontispiece:
This northern appetite – this *bon viveur* –
This bear-faced bevvying barnacle –
"B.V.", as he would have me style my poems.

An umpteenth birthday passed in a cage of rain;
My small perennial hopes – a collie, and heather,
And Harriet Barrs – were ash in the grate again;
So when he knocked and wheedled and begged and beavered
And roared to have our head, my self was spent,
And he dissolved us in his element.

But leave that – since the terms of my new estate
Are to walk as I have never walked before!'
So we did walk: he streets ahead, composing
a queer Senecan hopscotch, or drifting
beside me in companionable silence;
until the dark began to fade.

Then he pulled up, as if short of breath,
and seemed to be sweating, and needed a shave,
and offered his empty hand in a hurry,
'I leave the card of *The Rambler* magazine,
as I cannot be sure of my present address
for some time to come,' and was nothing.

NOTE: *The story of the poet James Thomson (1834–82), author of* The City of Dreadful Night, *is told in Tom Leonard's book* Places of the Mind. *Thomson was born in Port Glasgow but removed aged six to London, where he was educated in an institution for Scottish orphans. An alcoholic, he was 'discharged with disgrace' from his first post as an army schoolmaster, and thereafter lived as a lodger in a succession of single rooms in Pimlico, scraping an irregular income from contributions to journals like* Cope's Tobacco Plant. *He never published under his own name, preferring the pseudonym 'B.V.' and in one fit of self-disgust burned all his personal papers as he approached what he wrongly thought was the midpoint of his life, his thirty-fifth birthday. Twelve years on, offered a belated chance by friends, the Barrs (two brothers and a sister), to recover himself in the Leicestershire countryside, he relapsed instead into one last 'dreadful night' in the city, and died of a broken blood vessel in his bowel a few weeks later. He was an uncompromising free-thinker, and a constant theme of his serious verse is the impossibility of an afterlife.*

III

... which have no memorial, who are perished as though they had
never been
    – Ecclesiasticus

Tonight I saw, concerning the Milky Way – a phenomenon we have
understood as a form of a vapour, raised to reflect the glow of the
stars in their houses – this contrary characteristic: it is crowded, and
each part crowded again, with its own infinitely progenitous rabble
of living stars. Neither – unless it were calculated elsewhere that we
should devise such a chamber of lenses as is our instrument today, by
the seemingly random development of optical science in Antwerp – is
this rude theatre set up for the instruction or amusement of mankind.
For my observation suggests what may be impossible to conceive
except by figure or metaphor: that our Zodiac is like a false vault in
the cellar of Babel: whose brightest lights, in the vast upstairs, would
disappear.
    – GALILEO, Notebooks, 12 June 1611

It's a free-for-all. Vandals have shattered the Sistine ceiling
and pitched the creator down on the midden with Castor and
    Pollux;
and the notes of the scale are heard no more, nor lanterns
    seen
than the holes between; or the wide estates between holes,
where heaven's unlikely guest revolves at his massive leisure
or bores his way through sleeps of aether; where the worst,
    fractious
asteroid beams in her thousand miles of cold dominion.

And fair play to rejects – to busts with broken noses –
whose last great work was finding a shed or a stable to die in,
if they dream away their loss of face in a sky like that;
if there, though day's glare or the northern night obscure
    them,

though nature has done with them, still through the void they
   hurtle their wattage,
powered with the purpose of having been – being, after all,
   stars,
whose measure we may not take, nor know the wealth of
   their rays.

Unpublished and Uncollected Poems

from The Counties of England

Middlesex

Something too small has tried to creep into the party.
It is covered in smog and carries the *Evening Standard* –
Everyone giggles. Up goes a rustic bouncer.
Then out of its pocket the midget uncrumples a postcard
Insisting, 'I'm terribly sorry, but I *am* a county';
Nobody talks to the thing, and it leaves at the end.

Nottinghamshire

The home of lace, where public servants act
As though their heads were made of the same stuff;
Where else would they hold up the London train
For fifteen minutes, just to look for a trinket
One old lady *might have* left on it:
'A black plastic cup for poaching eggs'?

Westmorland

Fragments of weather-war. A frost in May
Searing the damson blossom. Hay uncut,
The know-all cocking looks at Morecambe Bay
Where indigo clouds trundle from beaten Ireland.
Late August: oats which swam in the June wind
Laid in bleak patches, mottled, grey-green, drowned.

Wiltshire

Sitting astride a Chieftain's gun-barrel today
I imagine a plain near Avebury, and a soldier
Repeatedly raped by a circle of virgins disguised
As old rocks. Colleagues are working on similar scenes
To be set in a Chippenham shop selling woollens and tartan,
At Marlborough School, and in sundry Victorian houses in
    Swindon.

Solomon

We must have hinted our desire . . . At once
The imperial guard of eunuchs scrambled out
To hoist our standard over remote quarries
And work our summons in the virgin seam.
As if a great magnet suddenly played on it,
Earth's surface ached – and soon, what trickled up
Invisibly, in secret tributaries,
Swelled to a general and an inward flood;
Until, from the Torrid Zones and frigid Poles,
From giddying scarpways and the viprous marsh,
From poultry farms and paddyfields, over
The convent wall, and through their father's clutches,
With a rapt religious purpose, there converged
To crown the whole horizon where they came
A tightening circle of exquisite girls;
On foot, on horseback, some on camels, some
On crutches, others crawling, all compelled
Like eastern kings, by my will's hanging sign,
To pitch their tents about Jerusalem.

A world of wives! – The colours of the map
Encamped as on the acres before heaven;
And every day I'd venture in fresh fields
To add unknown sensations to the spectrum;
For each submissive blonde was her own shade,
And no black would repeat her neighbour's hue,
So every Sabbath I could call to view
A startling rainbow arched over the week
Whose seven elements combined anew,
As sun meets shower, in brief entanglements

Designed by Solomon. This way my palette
Flourished, like Adam's lexicon of beasts,
Somewhere between a paint-box and the zoo.

I rarely asked a name. A woman's soul
Appeared to me, and is retrieved by me
In terms of colour. Names have unwieldy,
Shared, defective, ageing histories
Betokening much beyond the split second
A sexed animal needs to express herself.
For instance: when the *English* come to mind,
I see the blush of little pastels wrapped
Like apples in a basket, and remove
Layers of reserve like linen, to let breathe
Cathedral greens; the brass of trumpets blown
Through blazed cheeks; stipple winking from a pond;
Blood on the dairy floor, and the rum buff
Of broken pots in sheds; the pebbled blue
Of a spring sky; the quick flare of blue
Skimmed by the kingfisher through evenings dim
With dying bonfires . . . wet dawns, dripping mint,
A freckled spawning, and a sense of moss
On the inside of things, and rust, and gloom.

So much for England, then. And so it went –
Till after the fortieth carmine, after the hundredth
Clichéd rose, and all the tract between,
A wish grew, to make monumental sense
Of all I'd known. That Sunday I conceived
The mural tribute to my million brides:
Whose rainbow shape would span the pearly start
And purple end of chromatography.
A life's work! Just the pencil line, a bare
Chainmail of nipples, inched across the void,

Cost weeks of cramp; but when it came to *paint* –
Was it the brush that couldn't register
The fine distinctions it was loaded with,
So many dates and skins and faces dried
Into one stain, for all I did with them?
Puzzling, I called an artist in, who sighed
And cuffed bits of spoilt pigment from the wall:
Colours (he lectured me!) *blossom apart,*
But they corrupt each other – mix 'em up,
You're bound to get the same, dull, mineral brown.
(Which set me thinking, how my single mind
Had come to fuse the bright particulars
That women brought, in a brown, saming fog;
And yet, my habit overruled my sense,
Or sense my judgment, and each daily day
Boredom got up and smacked me in the face.)

Sometimes it seemed a mixed lot – never to know
The simple conjugation of the mass
Of choiceless men and women – *he* and *she*
Boarding each other like a bus in sunshine –
Snug in the mouldings of their married berth
They sleep together now, like slotted bolts.
But who on earth governed a sum of parts
Equal to mine? – The Queen of Sheba? – She
Aspired; and for a game, tenacious month
Fought not to shiver in the freezing gulf
Between her fairness and my given greatness.
We even laughed together when she framed
Her woman's riddles on the abacus
(What has ten holes, that when the first is shut
The other nine are opened? – Though at once
I knew both answers, my reply of choice

Was to let these fingers irresistibly
Confound her reckoning.) How the subsequent
Dependence wore her charm away, until
We only had her leaving left – what else?
You'd find her weaving now, in a seaside town,
An umpteenth set of hangings for my bed
– Which will be beautiful, like her, but show
No clear improvement on the ones before.

Hero and Leander

Leander of Abydos, the champion youth
Of Asia Minor; Hero, our heroine,
Priestess of Venus at her easternmost,
The shrine at Sestos. Europe and Asia once
Had married here: divine sectarians
Had interposed the swirling Hellespont,
A no-man's-land between such boys and girls.
Their parents knew, and loathed, their opposite,
Different in all but that; their acid feud
Poisoned the straits between. How bright Hero
And proud Leander ever came to meet
Is thus mysterious; but having met,
They had to meet again. But how, if not
By open boat; and never at all by day?
How else: Leander swam the stretch by night,
His stroke set on the simple lantern tower
Where Hero watched, and where she nightly found him, –
Naked and wet, – and when he scaled the wall,
Shaking and breathing at her window-bay;
She let him in, and tried to keep him warm.

So for a month those perfect lovers loved,
Secret and safe, until their sliding stars
Revolted from them, and the weather went.
Then seven days and nights, storm beat the straits;
Waves heaved at the clouds, and heavy clouds
Breasted the waves to bomb the waves with tons
More water. Sodden and fearful, Hero wept;
Her lover, meanwhile, stormed more than the storm,
And as his Hero stood or lay at Sestos,

He could not bear to wait in Abydos;
At last, though moon and stars hid in their doors,
He threw his luck into the mile of black,
Which filled his lungs and stomach all at once,
And after a round of pitch and toss spat up
His blenched and bloodless corpse on Sestos shore.
That night Hero could hardly sleep, she felt
Such a foreboding: until before cock-crow
Catching a slumber, she dreamt the pair of them
Were playing checkers on a board of pearl
With pebbles at the bottom of the sea.

Her waking sight: Leander's carcass laid
Among dead fish there on her lap of shore.
At which a boisterous rack of tidal ridge
Ran in, and dragged him from her. Piteously
She strode in after to complete the wreck,
And the waves closed over her loving head.

Note on the Unpublished and Uncollected Poems

'The Counties of England' is a sequence of 39 six-line poems, each devoted to one of the 39 counties of England, that was published in *Poetry Review* (Vol. 76, No. 1/2, June 1986) under the pseudonym John Bull. Half of these were composed by John Fuller, and half by Mick Imlah. Eight of those composed by Imlah were included in *Birthmarks*. The texts of the four additional poems included in this selection are taken from *Poetry Review*.

'Solomon' is published here for the first time.

'Hero and Leander' was published in *Oxford Poetry* XIII.2, December 2009, a special issue dedicated to Mick Imlah.

MF